Cut
of the
Real

INSURRECTIONS:

Critical Studies in Religion,
Politics, and Culture

INSURRECTIONS:
Critical Studies in Religion,
Politics, and Culture

Slavoj Žižek, Clayton Crockett,
Creston Davis, Jeffrey W. Robbins, Editors

The intersection of religion, politics, and culture is one of the most discussed areas in theory today. It also has the deepest and most wide-ranging impact on the world. Insurrections: Critical Studies in Religion, Politics, and Culture will bring the tools of philosophy and critical theory to the political implications of the religious turn. The series will address a range of religious traditions and political viewpoints in the United States, Europe, and other parts of the world. Without advocating any specific religious or theological stance, the series aims nonetheless to be faithful to the radical emancipatory potential of religion.

For a list of titles in this series, see page 185.

Cut
of the
Real

SUBJECTIVITY IN
POSTSTRUCTURALIST
PHILOSOPHY

Katerina Kolozova

FOREWORD BY FRANÇOIS LARUELLE

COLUMBIA UNIVERSITY PRESS   NEW YORK

Columbia University Press
Publishers Since 1893
New York   Chichester, West Sussex
cup.columbia.edu
Copyright © 2014 Columbia University Press
Paperback edition, 2018

Library of Congress Cataloging-in-Publication Data
Kolozova, Katerina.
   Cut of the real : subjectivity in poststructuralist philosophy / Katerina Kolozova.
      pages cm — (Insurrections: critical studies in religion, politics, and culture)
   Includes bibliographical references and index.
   ISBN 978-0-231-16610-2 (cloth)—ISBN 978-0-231-16611-9 (pbk.)—
   ISBN 978-0-231-53643-1 (e-book)
   1. Poststructuralism. 2. Feminist theory. 3. Realism. 4. Gender. 5. Laruelle, Fran-
çois.   I. Title.

B841.4.K65   2014
199'.4976—dc23   2013021560

Cover image: © plainpicture/C&P
Cover design: Lisa Hamm

To my father

CONTENTS

FOREWORD: GENDER FICTION

FRANÇOIS LARUELLE

TRANSLATED BY ANTHONY PAUL SMITH

THE REINTRODUCTION of gender (an old notion from biology and the natural sciences) into the margins of sexuality has functioned as a redistribution of givens and interests; it has opened up [*libéré*] the field of thought at the same time as it has introduced confusions and polemics into it. Gender has become the new scene [*lieu*], the new enclosure [*enceinte*] that is necessary to think, and the problematic that is possible to work through once again. Katerina Kolozova boldly takes her place in "gender studies" with a look toward what I call non-philosophy. Her work is all the more interesting to me because non-philosophy's first and final word concerns the human as "generic," which I oppose to the metaphysical and even to the philosophical; we will come to understand why. I would like to suggest, for her line of thought and my own at the same time, the schema of a "non-standard" conception, not of the sexes, but of genders insofar as they include, extend beyond, and run through the classical distributions of sexuality. The metasexual dimension of gender is affirmed here; one may even want to say "non-"sexual if the usage of "non-" were well understood as a partial negation of what is dominant and harassing there, in a word, what is "sufficient" in theories of sexuality. Let us assume that psychoanalysis (without saying anything about sexology and its related disciplines) is guided by a *Principle of Sexual Sufficiency* (PSS), one of the modes (the dominant one though there are others) of which is heterosexual sufficiency. Here "sufficiency" is not a psychological and moral concept;

these are an effect, and they are hardly ontological. Rather, this is the critical thesis (the dualysis) that every notion of a philosophical spirit is surreptitiously assumed sufficient for itself and for the real that is being thought. For this the philosophical spirit is redoubled or reflected in itself, forming a double with itself, assertion, and reassertion; in this way the philosophical assures itself of itself against the hazards [*hasards*] of the real. So we must admit that the philosophy of sex and even psychoanalysis are the blending-together of reflected or amphibological notions that do not manage to determine their object precisely (even its indeterminate character) *but which believe that they can.* Within these conditions, which are its own, gender risks remaining a universal generality, an Idea, an imaginary center, even and especially when gender is divided by sexual difference or sexual duality folded in on itself, whether straight or bent or oblique. This is today's theoretical slogan, which replaces the "sexual-whole" [*tout-sexuelle*] and which can bring together different practices but not give the science of sexuality a concept that is a bit more rigorous and human. Too much idealism, too much materialism and empiricism: to be completely frank, a bad indeterminacy where the concept is itself without rigor and is believed for all that to be even better for getting to the real of sex.

How can the PSS be cut down except by a new practice of gender, which would abandon its conditions for existence, the doublets, and its general structure of division. This would be necessary to be able to speak of a generic science of the sexes, of their genericness as humans (and therefore its extension to nature). Man is not a "sexual animal," to parody an old definition, but a generic animal and maybe even gender par excellence insofar as man is an animal. It may be that this inversion will be interesting if it is no longer interpreted under philosophy's norms. It is under this condition that the generic no longer forms whatever predicate but rather "nature = X," that humans are sexed and can just "maintain" sexual nonrelations. There are no generic relations but rather another organization of the phenomena of sexuality. In other words, "sexed gender" will be the final element, autonomy, or completion of sexuality. A non-standard conception, which is a truly generic conception of "gender" itself, which recognizes the mark of the real, would arrange the givens in this way. Avoiding thinking either in positivist terms about sex (anatomy, physiology, sociology) or within the horizon of the empty Idea of gender is necessary. We need to add to it another, more rigorous method than the philosophical one, but without denying it. The method will be pulled from the quantum model, a protoquantum lightened and reduced to the most fundamental principles of quantum theory. Sexed gender is a special duality by virtue of its quantum nature; it has the structure of a complementarity of gender and sex but it is unilateral or nonreversible. The all-powerful sex does not determine an abstract "man" (PSS); rather, it is the inverse and yet otherwise than inverse; humans as generic or lived desire determine and even "underdetermine" sexuality. "Genders" only exist insofar as the two aspects are inseparable through the force of gender and separable from the perspective of sex, which must in its omnipotence be made low or underdetermined.

We will treat these genders as variables or properties of generic humanity. This inserts them into a matrix like the kind Heisenberg developed but which is adapted to human sexual materiality. As quantum, it only arranges the variables that are materially [*matérialement*] sexed (lived), and so they are indexed in an algebraic way, they and their products, by an imaginary or complex number. The matrix first implies conjugating these two variables and drawing two inverse products, but its quantum destination equally implies that these variables (the "sexed genders") are all vectors: they are the phenomena of vectoriality and no longer the phenomena of things or events in themselves or things that are "macroscopic." It is essential here to abandon the sex-thing (the organ or object, as well as the symbolic object like the phallus or object-image) and to think a sex-vector, a human and dynamic vectoriality rather than a macrosexuality.

Beyond the classical duality of sex and gender, sexed genericness passes through several phases or assumes properties that draw out the major lines of a possible "science of lovers."

(1) Sexed genders, in whatever manner that they exist, are like those a prioris that filter and inform sexual experience; they are linearly superposable, which means that a man and a woman add their lived desires [*vécues de désir*] algebraically as imaginary and are not identified by them. The desires or lived experiences of sex superpose themselves in the wave of a unique desire that can superpose with itself another desire; nothing excludes itself here; everything penetrates itself once each time. Desire is an insurrectional impulse [*élan*] within desire, an ontovectorial push that joins bodies, seeming to complete itself each time but without shutting down or closing upon itself.[1] Desire is "ascendental" from end to end and not "transcendental"; it does not exceed or overcome a transcendent being in the manner of a transition [*passage*], a leap or becoming between two instances or two multiplicities (as in Deleuze), but it is crossed through as if by a tunnel effect.

(2) But moreover, the bodies or organs that bear sexuation do not absolutely or completely vanish in the desiring flux without reconstituting even more a full body corresponding to desire. The bodies or organs are worn and made, guided and transformed by this drive when they are cast as a body in itself within the wave of desire that seizes it immediately. The desiring transformation of bodies signifies their loss of sufficiency or return to itself, the abandoning of their specular structure of doublets, which makes their closure macroscopic, a transformation that marks their fall into insurrectional immanence and opens up desire. Regarding the bodies institutionally individuated by philosophy, they lose their united and closed form and their autonomy, even that of the organs. They deconstitute themselves as if through a quantum and sexual deconstruction rather than through a textual one. Desire is only an undulatory phenomenon when it borrows the quantum "logic" of the quarter or the square root of -1. So it is less molecular or less a partial

object than a "quarterial object"; perhaps this is a way of understanding Deleuze's n-sexes. If there is a material and formal genesis of the waves of desire, then it is not the Idea (of Deleuze and Badiou) through which the divided subject-bodies engender themselves through metaphysical deduction or even a topological one. They are algebraically reduced to the state of a quarter or a half of their anterior unity, losing their locality and forming an entanglement that is the real content of primary narcissism. Bodies floating without the heroism of lovers, before calling for the closure of *jouissance* and the return of institutional harassment.

(3) The desiring flux, as undulatory, is not "cut up" by the bodies that it passes through; modernity and postmodernity have misused the cut and the multiplicity of cuts, using them as if they were openings [*premières*]. On the other hand, the flux is not commutable with the particles that it passes through. Just as the sexed genders or vectors that constitute it do not overlap each other, they are not commutable; we are not exchanging one desire against another or against pleasure—they are superposed. Though perhaps *jouissance* exchanges desire against pleasure.

(4) Sexed genders are evidently not themselves individuals but form a formalism known as material and not materialist. They are algebraically structured according to a regime of idempotence; neither analytic nor synthetic, their logic has nothing of the formal void, and moreover they are weaved within the neuter materiality *of a void, itself non-sexual, of sexual desire.* This second-degree formalism has as a "metasexual" function (meaning human in the last instance) resolving the antinomies of the philosophical interpretations of form and matter, or more exactly those of the logico-formal and materialism.

(5) Two sexed genders, if they can superpose themselves and form a new, well-defined entity, are not predicates or properties that both refer to the same object or direct it so as to exhaust its definition; the order of their intervention modifies their destination; they are not predicates that can be said about the same and unique object, of man in general defined by an essence or a dominant predicate. An indetermination is

admitted here of the generic real, the definitive abandoning of determinism and realism or what remains with the current dualities of sex and gender.

(6) We have delayed as long as possible the arrival of sexual difference (in the classical sense) on the scene, but it covers and colors—or "colors over" [*encolore*]—the overall generic apparatus that we have first constructed for man-in-person independently of its sexual specificity. Sexual difference, with its modalities, ties, crossings, seems to dissolve in the genericness of desire but finds itself transformed, at least within bodies. Properly speaking, the sexuation of gender is a trait that is not secondary but at the very least is complementary to genericness or included within it under the form of the becoming of bodies. What intrinsically makes the generic human specific, along with its proto-quantum rules (superposition, noncommutability, entanglement, or nonlocality), must be defined and modulated by the inevitable sexual language-bodies that a theory must finally adopt; it is impossible to remain within an asexual formalism even if such a formalism is the condition for the emancipation of the sexes. Is there a feminine use of superposition or a masculine one for entanglement, meaning a sexuation of quantum algebra itself? Is the use of these rules, if they are put into play with regard to sexual phenomena, already, for example, feminine-oriented or masculine-oriented according to the kind of individual and philosophical subject that serves as the material for the production of a particle? The solution will consist in recognizing that sexuality is generic-oriented or human-oriented through its essence and for all that it is even already fading [*déclinante*] from its dominant position, but there are different ways to knock it off its pedestal. If we take into account its bodily supplement, then the Human-in-person, even if it is sexually indifferent to a certain extent, is still only indifferent radically so, not absolutely. If sexuation does not directly codetermine Man-in-person, it is still an occasion and motivation. The debasement of PSS is only possible in two conjugated ways, principally through the desiring underdetermination of sexual sufficiency in general, and occasionally

through the original sexuality of the "philosophical" subject that acts. Finally, generic human desire and sexuation are not commutative; they form a unilateral complimentarity within which the first underdetermines or underempowers the second, which fades [décline] from its dominant position which is for us within psychoanalysis. But that fading is specified and motivated according to the sex.

(7) Finally, it becomes possible for the determination of the *queer*,[2] which seems to sit awkwardly with the classical sexual distributions, to be reappropriated, provided that it is inserted into the generic matrix and its conceptual and effective levels are changed. Sexed genders are affected by the imaginary number that is the condition for vectorality, the matrix itself, or the knowledge of generic matrix that is entirely [*globalement*] indexed on one such number, somehow inclined by the generic humanity that we have called the fading or disempowering of sexual sufficiency, which is not its negation and no longer a simple subtraction but its transformation. What is the relation with the queer? This final concept is related, or often interpreted as related, to that of *transversality* (as in Deleuze, Guattari, and Foucault), destined to collide with the Cartesian rectangular coordinates of philosophical space and to trace the complex sexual becomings there. But, as complex and hazardous as they are, they retain a final frame of reference in the simultaneous duality of the sexual genders' frame of reference; they are perhaps becomings that are infinite or unlimited but predictable and able to be discerned, in some sense philosophically calculable. "Transversality" provides us with a supplementary nuance to "trans-cendence," the version or "tending" [*verse*] (the operation of tending [*verser*]) that at the same time carries out a "trans-"cendence, a transition or leap that tends to go from one instance to another, so as to flow past.

Now what we have called the inclination or slope, which is assured algebraically, carries out a certain "dis-inclining" [*dé-clin*] of sufficient or corpuscular sex. This is even a version or an act of tending toward or even a transition, but one that is not reabsorbed in itself, that is not

closed upon itself and an *ad quem* instance or an object in itself. It is a
vector; it has a departure point, a transition point in which it provision-
ally completes itself, but not an arrival point where it would shut itself
away. This is a new concept for the *queer*, no longer Deleuze's n-sexes
for a sexuality of the "full body" that is virtually infinite, but a sexual
complementarity, a gender unilaterally sexed within every identifiable
sex, a transfinite or vectorial queer. It seems possible to us in this way
to extract the nuance of the queer from its traditional philosophical
context—to remove it from that frame and bring it back to a humane
or generic level.

ACKNOWLEDGMENTS

I WOULD like to thank my editor Creston Davis for convincing me to rewrite an old manuscript and resuscitate it into a new book we called the "Cut of the Real." It is thanks to his encouragement that this book stands before us now. I owe my deepest gratitude to François Laruelle for his friendship and for his support of my work through our occasional exchange of ideas. I would like to thank Nicola Masciandro, Michael O'Rourke, Anthony Paul Smith, and Paul Levi Bryant for their valuable recommendations as to how to improve and enrich the manuscript. Also, my thanks go to Clayton Crockett and Wendy Lochner for their support and advice throughout the process of preparation of the manuscript. In drafting the first version of this manuscript, my friend Ray Brassier has been a great help in my efforts to formulate concepts as clearly as possible in a language that is not my mother tongue. This process has been harder than all others that preceded it because of the vocabulary, which relies primarily on Laruelle's non-philosophical terminology.

The support of my friends and family in the process of writing has been very important to me. So I thank Kristina Kolozova-Antović, Artan Sadiku, Svetozar Antović, Mitko Cheshlarov, Roland Hennig, Isidora Hennig, and Senka Kolozova.

Finally, I would like to express my deep appreciation for the research grant and the support of the publication provided by the RRPP program of Fribourg University, Switzerland.

Cut
of the
Real

INTRODUCTION

1

One of the trends that has marked the past half decade in twenty-first-century continental philosophy is the emergence of several new forms of philosophical realism that are habitually (and perhaps problematically) put under the single label of "speculative realism."[1] This trend signals the need in twenty-first-century continental philosophy to traverse the postmodern or poststructuralist limits of thought. Paradoxically, "speculative realism" sees its limits in precisely the alleged "limitlessness" of thought it proclaims. Namely, it limits the ambition and desire of philosophical thought in three ways: (a) by contemplating the endless "chain of signification"; (b) with the critical theory of the linguistic auto-reinventions of the self (or "the subject"); and (c) and with the subversive reconfigurations of power within an established sociopolitical domain. These three basic limitations have thus outstripped the desire of philosophy and social theory of its core ambition, namely, the "reinvention of worlds." The position that the purported limitlessness of poststructuralist thought limits its interpretative and political ambitions is what unifies the otherwise inherently diverse current of thought that nowadays goes by the name of "speculative realism."

And the political problem of contemporary philosophy identified by the "new realists" is, in fact, the product of a more fundamental epistemic problem. In his book *After Finitude*, Quentin Meillassoux calls this problem "correlationism" and identifies it as an essentially post-Kantian legacy, which continues to dominate and limit philosophy. As a matter of fact, correlationism lies at the heart of postmodern theory and consists in the premise that thought can only "think itself," that the real is inaccessible to knowledge and human subjectivity, and that there is *nothing but* discursive constructs that fully determine thinking and that are methodologically accounted for all the way down.

Meillassoux claims that although the "out-there" is fundamentally contingent or chaotic and void of meaning, it still conditions our thought and invites us to "react" to it; indeed, he argues that the natural sciences are the proof of this "invitation." According to Meillassoux, if we take into consideration the model of scientific thought, we can easily conclude that "facts" are representations, concepts, or instances which aspire to be an accurate description of the reality. Yet this *representational*, or what François Laruelle calls a "transcendental," reality must also account for an instance that dictates the creation of the "fact" in the first place. This instance is called "factuality" (*factualité*) and is defined in the following way: "[the] non-factual essence of fact as such, which is to say, its necessity, as well as that of its determinate conditions."[2]

In his contributions to the exchange with Judith Butler and Ernesto Laclau in *Hegemony, Contingency, Universality*, Slavoj Žižek argues that it is the Real (in the Lacanian sense) that we ought to think nowadays, if we want a fundamental change in the political paradigm we live in. According to him, capital has assumed the status of the Real, and only if political thought thinks of a new Real rather than merely inventing relativizing playful subversions of it can we conceive of a fundamentally new political paradigm.[3] This implies that the Real is always grounded in the material, and it is for this reason that the Real is a status that can be assumed by other realities. The Real is not an abstraction, an idea that stands independently, an "out-there" in itself. It is not a substance, but a "status," as Laruelle would call it, a notion analogous to that of the "function" in Lacan.[4] Similarly, Badiou insists on the role of the "event" (a concept analogous to that of the Lacanian Real) as that instance of the "void" (a singularity without linguistic content) in relation to which new discursive possibilities are created. As Badiou says, "new truths are generated" by means of a "subject's fidelity" to the void.[5]

François Laruelle's realism is grounded in his claim that philosophy itself is the source of contemporary thought's self-circumscription and its paralysis in addressing reality, which would fundamentally change it or at least explain it with rigor. A rigorously described reality makes sense in other "doctrinal contexts" (schools of thought) as well. For example, science describes and interprets reality, Laruelle insists, in ways that communicate with a variety of theories, rather than only within a single and self-sufficient "universe of thought," as in philosophy. It is for this reason that Laruelle has often been inadequately labeled a "scientist" in philosophy and an antiphilosopher in the name of "science." Laruelle's most recent phase, his non-standard Christology, offers more proof of the inadequacy of the label of "scientism." Laruelle's non-philosophy or non-standard philosophy does not aspire to cancel philosophy altogether or replace it with science. The goal of non-philosophy is to rid philosophy of its dictatorship of the transcendental vis-à-vis the real, which again only leads to its narcissistic self-sufficiency. The first gesture toward this goal is the unilateral positioning of thought vis-à-vis the instance of the real. The Thought correlates with the real as the authority in the last instance rather than with a system of thought. In this way it operates with concepts that have been radicalized[6] and that are then used non-philosophically.

Here is a brief explanation of how the procedure of "radicalization" is carried out within non-philosophy. The non-philosophical process of describing and rigorously explaining a reality is one that observes the effects of the real, reacts to the "workings of the real" which resides behind the conceptual or discursive phenomenon that represents it, and builds its own syntax, which is then subjected to the real. This can be done only if philosophical systems are disorganized, rendered mere "transcendental material" or philosophical *chôra* that thought operates with, while succumbing to the authority of the instance of the real rather than to the authority of a philosophical system (or legacy of thought) or the authoritarian figure of a "thinker." For example, one can resort to and actively operate in his or her theorizing with the concept of "unilaterality" one finds in Deleuze, but one can do it without having to "become a Deleuzian" and use it only in ways that are determined by Deleuze's system (or "organized thought") as presented in *Difference and Repetition* and his other works. In order to accomplish this, one has to "radicalize" the term, that is, reduce it to its "transcendental minimum" or to the conceptual content that describes the workings of the real that have necessitated it (the concept), to its determination in the last instance. In order to arrive to the radical concept, thought has to correlate only with the real and in an immanent way (*de la manière immanente*) rather than with the entire conceptual apparatus of a school of thinking.[7]

Laruelle has demonstrated how these operations of non-standard philosophy can be applied to three doctrinal legacies, which, according to him, are minimally philosophical or as realist as possible: Marxism, psychoanalysis, and Christianity (when Christianity rids itself of philosophy and is grounded in the "figure of Christ" as a radical concept). The application at stake concerns the use of concepts in the interpretation of a particular reality. The fact that concepts of Marxian or psychoanalytic origin are used in the interpretation does not make the interpretation or its author automatically a Marxist or a Freudian, for instance. To his non-philosophical rendition of these three legacies of thought, Laruelle adds the prefix "non-," which stands for the distance from the dictation of "philosophy's self-sufficiency" and represents an affirmation of the instance of the real as the determination in the last instance of all rigorous theory. Hence, he writes on non-Marxism, non-analysis, and non-Christianity.

One important idea in Laruelle's theory is the "Vision-in-One," which refers to thought's unilaterally operating with philosophical concepts. This "Vision-in-One" is also called "nonrelational": it does not establish a relation that would define it with either traditional concepts or the real itself.[8] Let us reiterate: thought correlates unilaterally with the (indifferent) real but does not posit it; or thought is affected by the real or by the immanence,[9] but the real does not take the form of the meaning that is ascribed to it. As soon as it becomes a meaning, it retreats as the real. Moreover, it does not have to have a meaning at all, except in that unique and unilateral instance that is under a highly specific theoretical investigation. For example, in non-Marxism, the "human-in-human"[10] is seen as labor force, but it is labor force in the last instance only in the context of this particular theory. In short, the "human-in-human" (the radical human without humanism) as labor force *in the last instance* is a Vision-in-One only with reference to non-Marxism. It is not a general vision about the "essence" of the human or "humanity."

The Vision-in-One protects thought from becoming "unitary" or, in other words, from being the product of the unification of the real and thought. They are of an immanently different status and, therefore, the real cannot be reflected entirely by thought. However, the real is accessible to thought and there is an elaborated conceptual apparatus developed in the framework of Laruelle's non-standard philosophy that enables rigorous theory to be aligned with the real. The fact that postmodern or poststructuralist philosophy abandons any attempt to think the real by proclaiming it unthinkable only because it cannot be reflected by thought without a remainder betrays the old metaphysical desire for thought to possess (know, control, and take the place of) reality or the real. In other words, the real endlessly evades its total "translation," that is, the transposition into thought or language. So the postmodern canon has proclaimed the real absolutely "the unthinkable" and has declared the circular movement of thought thinking itself as the only relevant subject about which to theorize. The processes of endless discursive reconfigurations (or restructurings) have come to constitute the only reality worthy not only of theorizing about but also of even thinking. And this is so because linguistically construed reality is the only form of reality that can be subjected to thought's absolute authority and control. The pretension to absolute reflection, totally mirroring the thought and the real (that is, representation), discloses the old philosophical desire that the real be identical to "meaning." As a consequence, philosophy has assigned the real to "the being" of existence. The upshot here is that "thought = real" is replaced by "thought = thought." And so the problem persists because the "equation is still there," as Laruelle says.[11]

The equation produces what Laruelle calls an "amphibology" between thought and the real, which means they have become indiscernible from each other, forming a "mixture" that cancels in advance any possibility for a rigorous theoretical investigation.[12] In the last instance, the real cannot challenge the philosopher; it cannot *really* surprise her with some "meaningless" instantiation. However, it can surprise and confuse the scientist in a way deemed productive, and this state of confusion is a "legitimate" invitation for a deeper investigation. Philosophy, on the contrary, does not permit meaninglessness. It is erased in advance. The provocation of "something not making sense" is always already seen as a flaw in thinking that does not adequately conform to the founding premises of the school of thought a philosopher adheres to. The founding gesture of the philosophical "decisionism" is a tautology: the real cannot be meaningless because that would be meaningless. And the real as always the same meaning, the meaning identical to itself (that is, A = A), and so nothing different would emerge and the real would be forever frozen in static and unchanging terms. The real therefore becomes meaning per se. Consequently, the real turns into an instance of the transcendental. The real has been replaced and substituted by thought. Moreover, this substitution cancels out the real, resulting in the amphibology produced by the thought being "thetic" vis-à-vis the real.[13]

Let us examine how these moves hijack philosophy in terms of a few basic core concepts. Notice that concepts such as "the essence" and "being" are already an instance of amphibology between the real and the thought. "Being" is a philosophical idea in its origin, a purely transcendental product since it is a representation of meaningful reality or of the meaning of the real. In order to avoid the traps of amphibology, Laruelle suggests that the rigorous theory (of non-philosophy) refers to the "one" as one of the "first names" of the real. To the unilateral thought that does not wish to pass a decision (in advance) of what the real "in general" is, the real happens as a singularity that is thereafter rendered subject to a nonrelational, nonunifying theorizing. Therefore, it is a *theoria-en-heni*, or a "Vision-in-One."

2

Laruelle's non-standard philosophy proffers a conceptual apparatus and the possibility for a critical positioning of thought that enables me to undertake a radical critique of the mainstream legacy of poststructuralist feminist philosophy without abandoning it as a whole. Problems are addressed unilaterally, in their singularity, while retaining a position of accountability with respect to their context and a rigorous assessment of the conditioning effects of the context at issue. Amid the rich theoretical diversity called "postmodern and poststructuralist feminist philosophy," there seems to be a consensus concerning several binaries of asymmetrical opposing terms. One of the two elements of the binary is always negative and excluded (as meaningless) from the explanatory apparatus of what is deemed and recognized as postmodern theory of authority. It is excluded not only as meaningless, irrelevant, inoperative for the postmodernist and poststructuralist stance in interpreting reality but also as a politically reactionary and morally wrong notion. Here are several examples: (a) the one is always equated with totality, totalitarianism, and imperialistic universalism; (b) the real is the unthinkable and any attempt to think it is seen as a Cartesian pretension to defining the reality for the Other; (c) the only relevant reality is the one accessible to us and the one we live in, that is, linguistic reality is limitless in its (political) possibility and any discourse arguing for the productive reality of the limit is declared reactionary. For example, the endless expansion of a list of proclaimed cultural rights is seen as a priori positive, in spite of the fact that it could be done to the detriment of certain fundamental women's rights. The very ontology of limitlessness produces an epistemology and a moral dictate that occurs as its direct reflection.

In the book, I am considering these and several other asymmetrical binaries and oppositions of the same register. The three examples I have just presented aim to illustrate my claim that epistemology, ontology, and moralism form a hybrid that impedes the furthering of possibilities of contemporary feminist philosophy. The greatest potential for its "radicalization" and expansion of possibilities, I argue, lies primarily in the work of Judith Butler and Drucilla Cornell, specifically: (a) the political and interpretative potency in Butler's concept of "derealization" as a form of subjugation; (b) grief and mourning as means of political mobilization; and (c) Cornell's theory about the paradox of limit's (or limitations') creative effects (which I find analogous to the position of the real in Laruelle's non-philosophy or nonstandard philosophy).

I now return to the shared characteristics of the canon of postmodern and poststructuralist feminist philosophy that I critically consider in this book. Perhaps the central problem is the following: the claim for universalism is automatically policed by expunging it from any selfrespecting poststructuralist feminist philosophy. The chief reason for such (auto)censorship lies in the fact that any call for universalism is seen as a totalitarian appeal for silencing marginal voices, corruptively aiming for a hidden supremacy of a Western political model of emancipation. The "amphibology" of epistemology and political moralism always already excludes the possibility of conceiving of new forms of universalism that do not have to be totalitarian. And they do not have to be totalitarian because they do not have to be totalizing, generalizing, or "unitary" (in the Laruellian sense, as explained above). If we apply Laruelle's principle of "transcendentally impoverished" or radical concepts, we should be able to conceive of a radically universal solidarity. It will be a solidarity that unilaterally correlates with the real of women's subjugation and gendered violence. Thus, we will be able to speak of a universal that is not the product of a generalization or "unity of differences." Such a "universal," one that is not based on a particular civilizational model usurping the status of universality, is a nonreified purely categorical and minimally transcendental universal that does not cancel out its accountability for and to the particularities of different cultural, socioeconomic, and political contexts.

The radical or transcendentally impoverished concept is one that is not based on a *philosophical decision* about the real, a decision that institutes or substitutes the real, but rather on the "syntax of the real." The latter is a concept that appears in Laruelle's *Introduction au non-marxisme* and refers to a process that, in his non-standard philosophy, is also called "cloning."[14] Similarly to the process of scientific thinking, non-philosophical thought describes the real as rigorously as possible by allowing itself to be "affected by its immanence." Anything else would imply performing an essentially philosophical gesture of subjecting the real to a decision of what it (the real) should be in conformity with a particular "cosmology."[15] This procedure is characteristic of any and all philosophy, insists Laruelle, and it is what he calls "philosophical decisionism."[16]

The goal of this book is to conceive of possibilities of rethinking the real by building on the legacy of poststructuralist feminist philosophy and in particular a philosophy that is primarily grounded in the work of Judith Butler and her reappropriations of Foucault and Lacan. And this goal is not the product of a mere "philosophical desire" to introduce a "realist twist" to what is otherwise poststructuralism. What is at stake here is expanding the critical possibilities of a potent feminist philosophical legacy by affirming the relevance of theoretical investigations about the effects of the real on our discursive universes. Such a goal can be accomplished only by developing an adequate epistemological apparatus. The real, according to both Lacan and Laruelle, comes to being as the traumatic experience par excellence. I will argue that the trauma is not just an abstraction; it is not a mere generalization that always manifests itself in the same way and tautologically ("trauma is traumatic"). To the contrary, trauma has a multitude of instantiations, forms, and qualities of experience, and accounting for this experiential diversity matters. It makes a difference whether the trauma is caused by brutal physical violence or the loss of a loved one, or whether it is the effect of ("normal," that is, nonviolent) sexual experience. I will argue that it is important to describe the specific effects of these specific instantiations of the real and how they affect the discourse. In *Precarious Life*, Judith Butler describes the political potential of the experiences of grief and mourning. Concurring with Butler, I will add that the potential for political mobilization we find in the experience of grief is yet another argument in favor of the claim that the real has many "faces." Consequently, it is of great importance for contemporary feminist philosophy to explore and expand the epistemic possibilities of theorizing the instance of the real or the purely "experiential." It is this project that I embark on in this book, drawing on some of the major ideas in Butler's and Cornell's works. In this process, I resort to Laruelle's non-standard philosophy as the theory that provides the most effective epistemic tools for such a project, one without any remainder of or reference to the old realist traditions.

The "non-" that stands before the word "philosophy" enables subscription to the tenets of a specific philosophical tradition without committing oneself to its orthodoxy. The possibility of critique within a school of thought does not mean that its orthodoxy is surpassed. Orthodoxy, in its last instance, consists in the implicit and explicit ways of policing an adherence to a school's basic principles. It implies the ability to distinguish between what makes a thinker "one of us" and "one of them" (the philosophical "enemy"). This self-enclosure, or circumscription into a self-sufficient conceptual universe, is what determines orthodoxy in the last instance in spite of all the critique that might happen within *its boundaries*.

The means of non-philosophy have enabled me to think the real and conceptualize a form of realism that is not a reactionary gesture of nostalgic philosophical archaism. Rather, it represents an extension, supplementation, or expansion of the possibilities created by poststructuralist (predominantly Butler's) feminist philosophy. In this book, I conceive of the subject's grounding in the real while still adhering to the thesis about its linguistic constitution. Also, I have attempted to consider an instance in the "imaginary body" (the one Butler speaks of in *Bodies That Matter*) that functions as the real. I explain love in unilateral terms or in terms of "radical solitude." And I do this all by virtue of rendering poststructuralist feminist philosophical universes into unorganized "transcendental material" (the *chôra* Laruelle writes of). I theorize elements of this *chôra* from a posture of thought that is emptied from philosophical discipline and equipped with theoretical rigor stemming from the epistemic tools of Laruelle's nonstandard philosophy.

1

ON THE ONE AND ON THE MULTIPLE

PHILOSOPHICAL DUALISM: THE UNITARY AND THE NONUNITARY SUBJECT—A QUESTION OF "EITHER-OR"

An Introduction: About the Proscribed Names in
Contemporary Theories of Subjectivity and (Gender) Identity

Adherence to a determinate theoretical horizon provides one with the comfort and safety of philosophical certainty. It is a twofaced certainty established by the hybridization of the transcendental (or thought) and the real: the comfortable sense of unshakability in one's philosophical knowledge and the safe sense of "knowing the reality." Even when the proclaimed truth of reality is one of constant mobility, transformation, and instability, the stabilized truth of the reality forms a securely established reality from which one is reluctant to be sundered. It is that stability which one risks losing through a decision to "radicalize" one's critical position from within the "domicile" discourse (the school of thought one adheres go). By "radicalization" I mean getting to the roots of the discourse that has become one's theoretical inertia. Therefore, the use of the word "radical" is etymological.

"Getting to the roots," the "radical" theoretical position, at least the one argued for by this particular text, consists in questioning the content and mechanisms of autoconstitution and autolegitimization inherent in the founding conceptual constructs of a theoretical discourse.

Specifically, it would mean inquiring about some of the fundamental ideological-theoretical presuppositions that constitute the theoretical lineage to which one subscribes, those that virtually situate themselves as givens within and according to the discourse. It would be a matter of calling into question the putative truths that are removed from the ambit of interrogation, those that suppress questioning through mechanisms of discursive autolegitimization and that in fact function as axioms within that discourse.

With regard to the traditional genre classifications of the realms of truth-production (those that *disciplined* "science," "philosophy," "theology," and so on), I would like to remind the reader that science as a "genre" allows axioms to be questioned. The "genre" of philosophy, however, discourages the adherents of competing doctrines from tackling the questions that could undermine whatever doctrinal construction they may profess. Thus, the effect of undermining seems to be always and as a rule understood as destructive. In science such a gesture would be seen as one that brings forth and problematizes a fundamental aspect inherent in a conceptual construction without dismissing it altogether. In the philosophical practices of truth production, one can detect a repetitive and autogenerated instance of thought's self-censorship in the name of preserving fidelity to a certain discursive legacy.

Nevertheless, I believe that this sort of questioning from within of a particular discourse contributes to its conceptual vitality and to the reinvigoration of the doctrine it underlies. My aim here is to open up from within the discursive horizon of certain questions pertaining to the axiomatic structures that underlie the contemporary gender theory, which is predominantly poststructuralist. The aspiration that inspires this undertaking is not a pretension to getting ahold of the material truth out there and, thus, to rectifying the claims deployed on the basis of those problematic axioms. It is rather a desire to break through the inherent inhibitions of the doctrine, to liberate oneself from scholastic obligations and thus to defy whatever hinders the free and uncensored movement of thought.

From the outset, I am aware that the act of interrogating will itself be—to a certain consciously established extent—irresponsible, insofar as it abandons the stance of scholastic "responsibility" by striving to re-create a naïve state of wonder. The goal is not to attain definitive and irrefutable solutions, but merely to propose a few stimulating examples of questioning. Accordingly, the ambition is reduced to the mere exercise of an awakening of thought from the rigidity of doctrine. The aim is to produce an emancipatory move of stepping out from the scholastic enclosure that constrains the discourse of contemporary gender theory. This attempt to use theory to scratch the surface of some deeply ensconced ideational fundament may result *at least* in hinting at a radically new positioning of thought.

I would like to initiate this line of investigation by examining the status of an apparently fundamental presupposition within the poststructuralist and postmodernist (post-Foucauldian, post-Lacanian, and deconstructive) feminist theoretical horizon: that of the *essentially* nonunitary nature of the subject. The status, the conceptual content, and the immanent rules of discursive connections between some other fundamental distinctions are inherently related to the status of this claim within poststructuralist feminist discourse. So are those of stability and fixity versus mobility, of the one versus the multiple, and the real versus language, to mention just a few. Thus we arrive at my initial questions: Doesn't this proposition's very stability render it exclusive? Doesn't the stabilization of this particular truth introduce binary, oppositional, and dualistic thinking into the constitutive layers, into the very tissue of the discourse? My investigation will seek to focus on these and some other closely related questions, including that of the position of the instance and concept of the real vis-à-vis that of discourse and language. This question will impose itself as the central one.

The initial motivation for this theoretical endeavor originates, perhaps, more in the personal and experiential realm than in any intellectual or scholastic ambition to exercise and demonstrate one's competence in the domain of truth-production. My position at the outset of the investigation is that of one who has begun to feel uneasy about her existence as constituted according the dominant "postmodernist ideologies of being." The deconstructive promise of a never-ending textual and discursive (inter)play and the optimism of an unrestrained transformability of identity and freedom implied by the Foucauldian legacy are always already undercut by the impossibilities upon which these utopias reside. Namely, the playfully transformable existences of multiple identities are supposedly made possible by the impossibility of the one and the static, an impossibility professed by these ideologies (which in the years of my intellectual and personal formation had already begun to establish themselves as academic and intellectual orthodoxy); and it is precisely the fundament of an impossibility that gives rise to the aforementioned malaise. The impossibility of producing discourse about certain instances, such as the one, the real, the stable, and so on, creates irrevocable hindrances for thought. By being rendered "unthinkable," these notions introduce insurmountable aporias into the heart of the language at our disposal today.

This is another source of intellectual and existential discomfort. Resorting to celebrating paradoxes as the propagators of the postmodern era have done does not seem to me to have the intended effect. Praise of the paradox propagates yet another unending flux of the much praised unrestrained textuality. It gives me the impression of being a hysteric denial in the face of the obstacle (of the real). It reiterates the constantly reproduced linguistic reality by retreating to the infantile safety of the known in the neurotic oversaturation with discursiveness and textuality.

Thus, I would like to consider ways of overcoming such inhibitions and interdictions within the poststructuralist feminist discourse without diminishing the theoretical accomplishments and political advantages it has brought about. Let us tackle first the claim concerning the nonunitary nature of the subject which has attained the status of an axiom in poststructuralist and postmodern philosophy. The modal instance of nonunity seems to have achieved the paradoxical status of a certain defining substance.

The poststructuralist propagation of the idea and the installation of the reality of the nonunitary subject are inherently related to the insistence (of the same theoretical provenance) on the subject's radical instability. It relies on the premise about its inherent mobility, transformability, and multiplicity. The presupposition of the subject's essential instability is, in fact, the founding assumption, which enables the autoimposition of the axiom about the subject's nonunitary nature.

Let us consider the putative truth of the subject's constitutive instability and examine the initial contention of this discussion, namely, that this idea has always already been stabilized as a theoretical position by the discourse, which professes it. It seems that the claim concerning the subject's unarguably nonunitary constitution and "principle of being" is something that cannot be critically questioned within this theoretical horizon, except for the purposes of reasserting the same claim. Any other attempt is hindered by the self-imposed constraints of ideological correctness.

Could it be that the stabilizing factor is already inherent in the founding assumptions of those poststructuralist, constructivist, and deconstructive discourses? Could it be that the assertions about the nonunitary and unfixed nature of the postmetaphysical subject work as the stabilizing gesture of coming to terms with the sense of uncertainty (which has culminated in past years in the rise of the precariat instead of the proletariat)? Our guiding question can be differently formulated: might there not be some underlying conceptual structures, occluded by the very regulations of the discourse in and through which they exist, that remain beyond the reach of the theoretical approach upon which the concept of the nonunitary subject is based, namely, deconstruction?

The motivation for asking this question, for granting its relevance and legitimacy, becomes more apparent when we begin to notice to what extent this "postmodern" insistence on a nonunitary conception of the subject, far from diminishing binary oppositions, actively perpetuates a more insidious variety of dualistic thinking. Thus, the relentlessly self-avowed "postmetaphysical" position with regard to possible conceptualizations of the subject, insisting as it does on the subject's exclusively nonunitary status, allows as its only possible alternative that of the opposing metaphysically unitary and stable subject. Despite the poststructuralist insistence on nonmonolithic thinking in all significant feminist writing that advocates the idea of the nonunitary subject, any position that allows the possibility of a subject residing upon (any sort of) a unifying principle is by definition dismissed as metaphysical. It is also dismissed as oppressively stabilizing and totalizing. The problem lies precisely in the logic of this dismissal, which functions "automatically" and "by definition." (We will examine the evidence for this claim in the discussion below.)

Nevertheless, my intention here is not to argue against the poststructuralist and deconstructive critique of the ideal of the unitary subject, an ideal upheld by the entire philosophical (or "metaphysical") tradition from Cartesianism to positivism. First and foremost, it is important to reiterate that I find the core of this critique convincing. Indeed, it is simply one of my own axiomatic starting points. (I state my position here without the intention of entering into a scholastic discussion and defense of this conviction, which is of an axiomatic character for me. Such an exposition would lead to an entirely different investigation.) My thinking has been formed, or rather, I have been "intellectually raised," like so many of my generation, by the postmodern academic and political thinking of the authorities of the era.

Therefore, what I would like to problematize is solely and precisely the question of dualism: the binary and oppositional self-positing of poststructuralist theorizing that argues for the nonunitary nature of the subject. I will propose instead that the dichotomy between *either* an exclusively metaphysical and unitary *or* an exclusively nonmetaphysical and nonunitary thinking about the subject creates a vicious circle whereby each of the two mutually exclusive positions reciprocally generates its other.

It is precisely insofar as it posits itself in our "world" (of ideas, concepts, and linguistic availabilities) solely and exclusively according to this binary logic that the thought of the nonunitary subject situates itself as agonistic, oppositional, and exclusive with respect to other discursive possibilities. A meticulous survey of the seminal texts of feminist theory that proclaim their poststructuralist (or "postmodern") provenance will reveal the inflexible rigidity. Namely, in accordance with the rules governing the poststructuralist and postmodern philosophy, any contention in favor of (any sort of) unity for the subject must be summarily dismissed as metaphysical or reactionary. In fact, it will show the complete absence of any claim about the subject's unity in any instance, context, or sense whatsoever. In addition to this, it will reveal this discourse's constitutive inability to think the questions of unity, of the one, and of the real in a way that is not metaphysical. This discourse suffers from an immanent, fundamental, and insurmountable inhibition in the use of language when attempting to make reference to the self-evident fact of a certain force of cohesion within the subject. It remains reluctant to explore possible instances and configurations of unity, which is emphatically not a unity of differences, but of oneness and singularity.

Poststructuralist (feminist) discourse is vitiated by a debilitating lack of linguistic resources for tackling these questions. Moreover, its inability to address such issues without dismantling their relevance altogether and consigning them to the conceptual junkyard of metaphysical remnants produces the chief points of aporia in this form of discursivity. The utter lack of conceptual tools for conceiving of the subject's unity in a way that might be post- or nonmetaphysical underlies such celebrated paradoxes of postmodern discursivity as "one, yet— multiple: The one *is* multiplicity and the multiple *is* oneness!" But such paradoxical formulations continue to assume that the multiple is the truth of the one while refusing to acknowledge the converse. Multiplicity and nonunity are that which truly exists, while oneness and unity are fallacious, a mirage of a kind. Yet the question remains: could there be a poststructuralist, constructivist, and deconstructive critique of the

(Cartesian) unitary subject that could also and simultaneously allow us to conceive of the subject as residing in some mode of immanent oneness and stability that would not be a constrictive and exclusive metaphysical formation? Is it possible to conceptualize a subject according to some paradigm of unity that is not totalitarian, a subject of autotransformative oneness, of identitarian mobility, in short, multiple in one sense yet an instance of oneness in another? And could we conceive of both instances as immanent?

Within the horizon of discursive possibility proper to poststructuralism, this is a conceptual stance that should be both permitted and granted its minimal pertinence. It should be done so from a perspective that is methodological as well as political. But the grave linguistic hindrance identified still remains: namely, the critical lack of the conceptual tools required for such debate. The challenge is thus to undertake the task of creating a discursive basis for thinking unity (of the subject) in terms that are neither metaphysical nor totalizing. Thus the task we shall set for ourselves is to conceive of an instance of unity or oneness for the subject without dismissing the relevance of the poststructuralist discovery of the multiple and transformative subject. It is an even greater challenge to demonstrate how such a discussion might be neither contradictory nor deficient in theoretical rigor.

Conceptualizing Unity "After" Its Deconstruction

The concept of "unity of the subject" as we meet it in the poststructuralist, deconstructive, constructivist legacy of the critique of the unitary subject represents a peculiar synecdochic construct. Namely, it seems that the notion of unity necessarily implicates the traditional attributions of "totality," "fixity," and "exclusiveness." These are *pars pro toto* identifications that regularly appear in the form of a conceptual totality.

The ideological minimum of the "project of the nonunitary subject" is indebted in its greatest and methodologically most significant part to

Derridean deconstruction. However, this deconstructive critical composition seems to silently refuse subjecting itself to any deconstruction. In its domicile ideology, the conceptual structure of the fragmented, unstable, multiple, inclusive, and nontotalitarian subject has never been subject to radical critique insofar as it is a *structure* itself. This possibility is always already impeded by the axiomatic presupposition that the only standpoint of radical critique of the notion of the nonunitary subject is the one of the essential opposition of its perennial other, that is, the metaphysical position.

However, let us assume the possibility of a deconstructive look upon this conceptual conglomerate, which will reside in immanently deconstructive epistemic presuppositions. With this assumption made, what remains is to engage in a heuristic reading of the language economy of the discourse. Let us endeavor to reconstruct the traces of power distribution through acts of naming some concepts that are founding or central to the discursive constitution of the nonunitary subject. The principal question in this sense is: is there a term that holds a hegemonic position among the other key words within this conceptual complex?

I will argue that there is such a hegemonic term. In fact it is the empty place of a term, the absence of a name, the "Name of the One." The dismantled one presides over the subsidiary concepts of the dismissed totality, stability, autonomy, exclusiveness, and so on. In effect, they are the automatic deduction of the one; they are also its automatic reduction. Oneness is a priori reduced to "these sinister effects" of its eventual "reign" and, in addition to this gesture of aprioristic deduction, it is also reduced to its results. Hence, the autogeneration of the acclaimed postmodern synecdoche of the nonunitary subject. The one is normally conflated with its own "bad produce," first and foremost with the procedure of totalizing and, thus, universalizing. The subject as a possible one, or as the possibility of some unity for the subject, is unavoidably identified with the (Kantian) modern(ist), autonomous, self-sufficient subject of exclusion (with respect to the other). On the other hand, oneness as singularity is identified and conflated with seclusion and exclusion, implicating the sovereign subject of soliloquy.

Venturing into an ontological discussion over the one and the multiple and the dichotomy they form is not my intention here. Instead, I would like to address the question of the discursive exclusion and censorship of the "Name of the One." It seems that in the entire post- and antimetaphysical philosophical-ideological legacy, there is a tacit aprioristic expulsion and moral condemnation of any position from the perspective of the one and, thus, of the unity as singularity (not as differences). Both terms are inescapably related to and degraded by the notions of totality (and totalitarian repressiveness) and universality (understood only and exclusively as a thinking act of hegemonic universalizing).

Within this entire context of the anti-Cartesian critique of the unitary subject, the feminist constructivist and deconstructive theories of subjectivity seem to suffer from self-censorship regarding the very use of the Name of the One in the affirmative sense (or in even the sense that risks being interpreted as affirmative). There is both tacit and overt autoprohibition with respect to the possible operating with (or application of) any sort of logic of the one or thinking in terms of the one, precisely because of the axiom of postmodern antimetaphysics, according to which any theorizing that claims the reality of a certain one and oneness is a priori universalistic, totalitarian, exclusive, and so on. Thus, the place of the "one" in the signifying chain in the politico-theoretical language of the postmodern word (= the discourse) is an empty place.

I would like to call for a retrieval of the position of the "one" within language, the position that it rightfully owns, together with its legitimacy as linguistic reality. Moreover, this retrieval should be accompanied or even enabled by the simultaneous reclaiming of the "right" of the name (of the one) *not* to be identified in the aforementioned reductivist manner with the "universalistic" and the "totalitarian."

My contention is, thus, that in the feminist (and not only feminist) discourses of deconstructive critique of the unitary subject, the *use* of the term "unitary" is insufficiently examined in terms of its oppositional relation to the favored "nonunitary." Or differently put, it sometimes seems to be functioning as an almost magic utterance of condemnation, a sort of anathema of the nonabsolutistic era, since, in the discourses professing the nonunitary subject, the "unitary" automatically, that is to say, with no critical stance, with no intellectual pausing, also entails the notions of stability, totality, fixity, and so on.

The feminist critique of the unitary subject, traditionally defined (also by itself) as marginal in the landscape of the intellectual power-network, is already rigidified within its own position, and in such a way that it can only produce the pure opposition of its own constructed other. The position of its theoretical other is fixed and its conceptual content unchangeable. It is, as a rule, considered always already diagnosed by a certain instance of an internal autoregulation of the discourse pertaining to the "mainstream autonomy theories"; Marilyn Friedman writes, "Feminist philosophers have criticized mainstream conceptions of autonomy . . . those conceptions ignore the social nature of the self. . . . Mainstream autonomy theories assume that we should each be as independent and self-sufficient as possible."[1]

This is one among the myriad of examples of generalization of the kind that produces this eternal theoretical other *in* the contemporary feminist (poststructuralist) theories of identity and subjectivity. To Friedman, "autonomy theories" appear to be synonymous with "unitary subject theories" and the latter seem to be synonymous with "stable identity theories." She proposes the position opposite to "the mainstream autonomy theories," drawing on Judith Butler's conception of subjectivity: "Feminist criticism of mainstream theories of autonomy is that they presume a coherent, unified subject with a stable identity who endures over time and who can 'own' its choices. This presumption is challenged by postmodern notions of the subject as an unstable, fragmented, incoherent assortment of positions in discourse."[2]

Here one sees an example of that reductionist interidentification of several predicates. It is detectable also in the following quotation, in which one can also notice the inhibiting effect of this package of attributes that must all go together as one. The lines, taken from Rosi Braidotti's *Metamorphoses*, display that aporetic and inhibiting situation in which the argument in favor of the nonunitary subject is installed on the grounds of excluding the possibility of other, new, and nonmetaphysical forms of unity and coherence for the subject.

> Sexuality is crucial to this way of thinking about the subject, but unless it is coupled with some practice of the unconscious . . . it cannot produce a workable vision of a non-unitary subject which, however complex, still hangs somehow together. . . . I would like to point out, however, that whereas in the psychoanalytic tradition these internal crevices are often the stuff that nightmares and neuroses are made of, they need not to be so. I would like to take the risk of arguing that the internal or other contradictions and idiosyncrasies are indeed a constituent element of the subject, but they are not such a tragedy after all.[3]

It is precisely the exclusion and the suppression of the thinkable one that creates this situation. Braidotti embarks upon a courageous project to transcend or bypass this aporia, to establish some insight into the substance and the ways of that "glue" which holds together that "subject-which-is-not-one," without abandoning her poststructuralist position. She is attempting to accomplish this by resorting to psychoanalytic instruments of critique and to the notion of the unconscious.

Further on, just one paragraph below the one quoted, Braidotti takes all precautions not to betray the vision of the nonunitary subject, while she actually continues with her search for that which holds together that "bundle" called subject: "I take the unconscious as the guarantee of the non-closure in the practice of subjectivity. It undoes the *stability of the unitary subject* by constantly changing and redefining his or her foundations."[4] However: "Non-unitary identity implies a large degree of internal dissonance, that is to say, contradictions and paradoxes. *Unconscious identifications play the role of magnets, building blocks or glue.*[5] The latter statement leads Braidotti to the following one: "Following Irigaray, the most adequate strategy consists in working through the stock of cumulated images, concepts, and representations of women. . . . If 'essence' means the historical sedimentation of many-layered discursive products, this stock of culturally coded definitions, requirements and expectations about women or female identity—this repertoire of regulatory fictions that are tattooed on our skins—then *it would be false to deny that such an essence not only exists, but is also powerfully operational.*"[6]

If we decide to follow the argumentative line linking these several quotations together, we can see that Braidotti is not only in pursuit of that "thing" which glues together the "bundle called subject," that is, in search of its *unifying* "forces," "principle(s)." She also seems to grant a certain legitimacy to the notion of "essence." Thus, by *reinventing* the notion of "essence," she takes the argument even further in the direction of some idiosyncratic reclaiming of the instance of unity. This is a reinventive and idiosyncratic arguing for unity, since it is embedded in a position that is one of an advocate of the notion of the "nonunitary" subject.

Some might find Braidotti's position contradictory. However, it is not. Her line of argumentation and inference is impeccably logical and highly convincing. She is arguing for the existence of some unifying processes in a certain instance of the subject, whereby the subject itself is *ultimately* nonunitary. Moreover, her claim might not even be paradoxical, since it seems to be perfectly compliant with the norms of formal logic. Namely, Braidotti's argument, sublimated in the way I proposed, consists in the claim that the coexistence of unity and nonunity is made possible by the simple fact that the existence of each of the two rests on a different ontological level and represents a different, distinct epistemological moment.

What, in Braidotti's text, produces those rhetorical swings of overly alert vigilance regarding the possibility of being "misread" as someone who propounds an idea of subjectivity different from that of the poststructuralist notion of the nonunitary subject? In other words, we can trace an overt intention to *identify* with a particular theoretical "school," to self-identify as an advocate of a certain "truth" as propagated and defended by a determinate discursive community.

The open self-declaration of belonging to a determinate line of thinking (about a specific issue) within the same discursive and textual act (on virtually the same page) that contains a claim which can be interpreted as being in opposition to this declared belonging is a statement of disavowal of any connection with a different theoretical linage. It is an act of ideological self-identification and a statement of renunciation of any association with a different theoretical school. The repetition of the statement of self-identification is a performative act of self-subjection to a certain ideology—in this particular case, the poststructuralist one.

The defensive language of Braidotti's argument for (some) unity of the subject, reflected in those repetitive self-declarations, speaks of the importance bestowed upon the question of theoretical-ideological belonging. This cautious language is voiced most "loudly" in the little words such as conjunctions, adverbs, and so on, for example, in the "however" and "still" in the sentence "it cannot produce a workable vision of a non-unitary subject which, *however* complex, *still* hangs somehow together."[7] But it also speaks of the discourse's powers of inhibition with respect to the potentially free course of argumentation, the movement of thought.

On the occasion of a seminar devoted to her work and aimed at younger feminist scholars from Eastern and Central Europe, Judith Butler was asked by one of the students if the nonunitary subject, through its constant inconstancy, is not always already facing the question of "survival," the possibility of its death. At one point in this dialogue, Butler says:

And I do think that certain forms of social transformation do involve passing through the fear of death. And I don't think it's a bad thing.

And what's of course interesting about the fear of death is about who I am. I could say at a certain point in time, that this is who I am and I cannot imagine myself any other way. I will dissolve if I do x, y and z. I will become undone fundamentally if I do x, y and z. And then it turns out you do x, y and z, hopefully within a community in which others are doing the same, and indeed something in you is undone, or even dies. But there is some new possibility that also emerges in its place.[8]

In this quotation, the same tone of cautious rhetoric can be detected that prevents the speaker from falling into the metaphysical "trap" of allowing any possibility whatsoever for a unity of the subject. In a word, the transformative subject is but a social one, and this subject is called an "I" only when its possibility of "dying" or being "undone" is spoken about, which in this (Butlerian) context means when it undergoes a social change and, thus, expresses political engagement.

When the existential lacuna appears out of the absence of any (new) sociopolitical position, what reemerges in the place of the old "I" is not, in the discourse of Butler, some new "I" or different state or "nature" of the "I," but "some new possibility." Thus, in the lacuna of crisis, it seems as if there is no "I," as if there is no "I" of crisis, no "I" of the "space" between (different sociopolitical and cultural subjections), no "I" without the philosophically competent awareness of its social and political position, since, if there were any, it would be that "thing" which, in Braidotti's words, "glues" the subject together. If there were any, there should be some unifying principle presupposed. The a priori exclusion of any possibility of allowing a mode of unity within a concept of a subject that is in its ultimate instance nonunitary is, through its dichotomous restrictiveness, inhibiting of thought and pushes the discourse into the clench of aporia.

This is how even Judith Butler finds herself claiming something like this: "Think of the many years of Turkish migrant workers in Germany, for instance. A population that is not a citizen, that are not citizens, that are also not effaced from the view. Not absolutely absent, there, but spectrally human. They do not form part of the figure of what is human."[9] It seems to me that in the postmodern and poststructuralist discourse there is some tacit yet highly sturdy *prohibition* against thinking about the legitimacy of (let alone granting legitimacy to) a certain instance of a unity or mere exploitation of the "Name of the One" in affirmative connotation. The background of this prohibition is constituted by the unquestioned—or rendered as unquestionable—synecdoche of the unity with its unavoidable attributions of "totality," "fixity," "domination," "repression," and so on. Highly illustrative of this theoretical practice is the following quotation from Jane Flax: "The postmodernists regard all such wishes for unity with suspicion. Unity appears as an effect of domination, repression, and the temporary success of rhetorical strategies."[10]

Beyond the Dichotomy?

In order to enable the release of thought from the grasp of dichotomy, it seems necessary to grant oneself the right of disloyalty to the school of thinking one adheres to, since, as we have seen, it is the self-declarations of belonging to an "ideology" (or to a school of thought) that produce the positioning of thought which is exclusive and dichotomous. As for the poststructuralist theories, the belief that one is enclosed within one's own discursive horizon to the extent of being (self-)produced as a theoretical subject by and through the discourse itself only makes that constitutive exclusiveness insurmountable.

One of the possible approaches to the nonexclusive and nonoppositional theoretical repositioning is the critical situating of thought proffered by François Laruelle's non-philosophy. It consists in the simple gesture of radically stepping out of any sort of theoretical autoreferentiality. This means performing a doctrine-unattached leap of abandonment out of the enclosure of thought within the tradition of a certain discourse and the epistemological and political obligations of adherence. The leap itself, made on the basis of a mere "non-," one unequipped with the knowledge of any existing discursive grounding, is a leap of and into uncertainty. However, that act of stepping out, while producing itself, coproduces a discursive possibility of an unrestrained flow of thought.

Such a gesture of radical abandonment of any scholastic belonging is, however, not possible without a radical stepping out of the stance of self-sufficiency, of self-circumscription of a disciplinary field or discourse. The non-philosophy of François Laruelle professes such a gesture of a radical stepping-out with respect to philosophy and its narcissistic self-perception as self-sufficient, or, as Laruelle puts it, of the "principle of sufficient philosophy" (*principe de philosophie suffisante*: PPS). This is an attempt to undermine the autopositioning of philosophy based on "its being animated and entangled by a certain faith or belief in itself as the absolute reality, intentionality or reference to the real that it pretends to describe or even constitute, or to itself as the real itself."[11]

Therefore, Laruelle concludes: "This is its fundamental autopositioning, that which one could also call its autofactualization or its autofetishization—all that we assemble under the principle of sufficient philosophy (PPS)."[12] We should note at this point that in Laruelle's terminological apparatus the notion of "philosophy" and the notion of "the world" are interchangeable, synonymous. The term "the world" is used in a sense analogous to the notions of "discursiveness," "the language," "the transcendental," or "the conceptual world" of a society and a time. Without going any further into a technical explication of the nonphilosophical method of suspension of the "principle of sufficient philosophy" (PPS), let us only draw the analogy that the thinking subject's stance of loyalty in the last instance to a discourse and ideology implies the self-sufficiency of the discourse and ideology. Such self-enclosure of thought, a circular autocompletion resulting from the pretension to having consensually marked the horizon line of "the thinkable," is inhibiting for the authentically investigative thought.

In this vein, let us attempt to suspend the principle of discourse's self-sufficiency, let us endeavor to assume a stance of radically stepping out of the discourse we are subscribing to, which, in this specific case, is the contemporary feminist vision of the nonunitary subject. Let us thus allow the possibility that there might be a "good one," a "good unity," namely, one that does not necessarily have to exclude the multiplicity. In total, let us assume the possibility that both instances (of unity and of nonunity) can be part of the subject's constitution and simultaneously operative without being mutually exclusive. Let us assume that this "coexistence" is made possible by the very potentiality of the two instances to be operative on different levels within different structural subconstructs of the subject.

Before entering into any further reflection on this assumed "peaceful coexistence," let us briefly consider the question of our theoretical positioning in a "certain outside" of the dichotomy. Where is this position to be "located"? Or what constitutes it? If one assumes that the two do not create any division, that their simultaneous workings do not imply any exclusion of each other, the thought is then situated beyond duality. Duality always already implicates dualism, if it resides in the founding assumption that there is no possibility of thinking the two beyond their *relation* of two.

Thinking, however, beyond relation and relationism is thinking in terms of singularity. The minimal form of relationism is the binary. The situation of non-relatedness is one of radical solitude. It can only be the instance of oneness. This is a situation of thought in which even relations are being thought beyond relationism or nonrelatively. In other words, the reality of a certain relation, interaction is seen in its singular positivity. Therefore, the position of nondichotomous thinking is located in and constituted by the *one*, as one of the "first names of the real."[13]

The one I am attempting to (re)claim here, with the help of the epistemological apparatus proffered by François Laruelle's non-standard philosophy, is exempt from debts to any philosophical legacy. Any relation to such a legacy, any referring to a philosophical tradition of thought and its implication in our invocation of "the one," will inevitably render it totalizing and universalizing (totalitarian) or, conversely, particularizing. Since, the philosophical one, according to Laruelle, is always already unitary or a unity of differences.[14] Thus, let us venture to conceive of the one as an instance of the singular relieved from any historical (= discursive) responsibility, and within that very instance of singularity let us conceive of a uniqueness and a phenomenal and epistemic solitude. Furthermore, let us conceive of this singular position as absolved from any responsibility to be relative, that is, as void of the stipulation to be relational or to establish any relation whatsoever, since any sort of relationally constituted viewpoint is, in its minimal instance, always already a gesture of constituting a *couple* (with another concept). Coupling is binarism, binarism entails dichotomy.

Therefore, let us attempt to conceive of an instance that will preemptively undermine the process of coupling and the production of dichotomy, which is described by Laruelle in the following way: "The one is a *nonthetic* [*non-thetique*] Identity in general, that is to say, at the same time nondecisional (of) itself and nonpositional (of) itself: without will for essence [*sans volonté pour essence*], without topology for existence, without the contest for movement forth [*sans combat pour moteur*], without space or figure for manifestation. . . . The one is the transcendental minimum, the minimal petition of reality—that is to say, the reality presupposed by any petition in general."[15] Let us resort to the approach of thinking in terms of nonthetic oneness and suppose a unity within the subject that would be neither in an exclusive nor in an oppositional relation—nor, for that manner, in any sort of binary relatedness—with the subject's aspects of multiplicity and of nonunity. The assumption that there is an instance of unity does not exclude the presupposition that there are also instances of nonunity. In the paragraph by Braidotti quoted above, we read about the "bundle" (that subjectivity is) but also about the question of the "glue" that holds it together. Let us permit ourselves to ponder the idea of an instance of unity or oneness within the subject without the obligation to place it in any particular relation with the instances of nonunity. Such a relation would condition it, shape it, and act as an element of its constitution. Consequently, we will construe a relationally defined unity and find ourselves once again entrapped in philosophy. Therefore, let us attempt to think in terms of the "Vision-in-One" (as in Laruelle's work).

The "unitary subject" that we can invoke by drawing on the theoretical resources of François Laruelle's non-philosophy is not unitary in the sense of a cohesive unity of organized differences. Rather, it is a unity in the sense of the persistence of "a certain one" of a stubborn sameness, underlying the identitary and subjective complexities nd transformations.

THE QUESTION OF (SUBJECT'S OR SELF'S) CONTINUITY: A POSSIBLE LOCATION OF ONENESS FOR THE SUBJECT OR FOR THE "I"

The Subject and the "I"

It seems that the theory of gender identity of predominantly poststructuralist or postmodern scholarship has inaugurated a furtive substitution of the name of "I" with that of the "subject."[16] By resorting to the *name* of the "I," I am not referring to any philosophical or theoretical tradition behind it. I am not even referring to a philosophical concept tout court. Rather, I am referring to a name containing the pretension to signifying the reality of the self as a totality encompassing all of its experiences.

When I say "pretension to encompassing all experiences," I mean a tendency toward conceptual appropriation of all experience, including that which is beyond the language, namely, the effects of the body and the effects of the real. In other words, I am referring to the naming of "I" in a sense (as) devoid (as possible) of scholasticism and erudition. I am referring to its principally infantile and most common and colloquial use. The notions of the "infantile and common use" of language (or common sense), the Symbolic and language are surely not immune to historic contextualization.

Let us regard the name of "I" as a position in language that has become a suppressed in contemporary feminist philosophy by its being substituted for the name "the subject." Let us consider what limitations are imposed on thought by the suppression at issue, as well as on the sheer rough experiences of selfhood that ultimately evade any reflection.

In the context of Lacanian psychoanalysis, it would be a methodological fallacy to attempt to substitute the concept of the subject with the name of "I" that refers to an imagined sum or totality of experiences. If one thinks only of that *tuché* (of the real) which only strikes the *automaton* (of the signifying chain) as if only to remind it of its sovereign rule and unattainable position, it becomes clear that it is simply impossible to conceive of such substitution. The subject is the effect of the signifier, while the real reveals itself only through its lack within and for the subject. Still the psyche undergoes the traumatic workings of the real. How can "I" refer to these experiences as mine if the name of "I" is not at my disposal? It also belongs to the territory of the real that "I" do not control. "I" am a mere function in the signifying chain. I am not "I." I am a subject.

In Lacan's technical terminology the names of "moi"/"je" subsists side by side with, as well as distinct from, that of the subject (*sujet*).[17] The notion of "moi," which is grammatically a declined form of "je," has a rather clear technical designation in Lacan's terminology. It seems that the use of "je" remains more vague and elusive and shifts from the technical to the colloquial. This possibility of the term's sliding is what makes it close to the common and nonerudite use. My claim here is that its theoretical or scholarly elusiveness is not a reason to strip it of the possibility of being at play in these or any other theoretical considerations.

The same kind of elusive workings of the name of "I" are to be found in Foucault's theme of "the care of the self" (*souci de soi: de moi, de toi*, and so on) or of a topos of resistance that seems to evade its placing in the structure of the subject in the strict sense of the word. It is always at work in his (or, for that matter, in Lacan's) writing whenever it becomes impossible for the term "subject" (*le sujet*) to cover the undiscovered, unexplored territories of the theoretically imagined self, which are not subjected to reflection.

Nonetheless, it remains a commonplace that both Lacan and Foucault (and their respective legacies) have performed an act of philosophical takeover of the position once held in the philosophy by the ego (or the "I") in the name of the subject. To conclude, my argument here is simply that this act of "dethronement" has its own lacunae and that they are symptomatic. Namely, there are remnants of the philosophically imagined self that are "untranslatable" into the notion of the subject as advocated by this theoretical legacy that is rather heterogeneous yet relatively in unison; moreover, it is precisely in the texts of the forefathers of what is nowadays known as poststructuralist theory that we find at play the elusive name of "I" supplementing or complementing that of the subject.

At this point of the discussion, I would like to propose going back to the question of the dichotomy of the unitary and nonunitary subject with an approach that integrates the aforementioned lacunae into the poststructuralist concept of the subject. The lacunae are the cracks of absence in the "voice" of "I," in the incapacitated and silenced uttering of an "I" that is too awkward and too inarticulate to substitute or fit into the conceptual structure designed for the name of "the subject."

Before we proceed, it should be pointed out that there is no clear-cut distinction between the notions of identity, subject, and subjectivity and the name of "I" in the considerations present in this book. In fact, every now and then, they will appear as interchangeable or act as synonymous. Their overlapping of meaning seems to be of a "metonymic" character, rather than a "metaphoric" one. The latter would imply interidentification consummating in a single identity or signifier that appropriates all the others, whereas what I have in mind is a meaning shifting across the terms, along the lines of their closeness, namely, a "sliding" in the naming that takes "place" along the borders that intersect the notions (or the names) in question.

Subject's Survival or the Continuity of an "I": Questions of "Location/s" of Perseverance

2.2.1

Even when conceived of as a continuous process of transformation, an instance of constant transformability and multilayeredness, the subject is, nonetheless and still, subject to and the subject of continuity. It is subject to a process of perseverance of an instance that provides the basis for a certain degree of unity of the transformable subject. The "subject" refers to itself by the name of "I" and it imagines itself as inescapably identical to itself. The importance of the question of "persistence and survival" is one of the central claims of Judith Butler in *Undoing Gender*. In this book we meet a plethora of examples that resort to the words "I" and "self," even though they are identical in meaning with the notion of "subject."

Continuity is perseverance of a certain "same"; this "same" is indispensable in providing the possibility of numeric unity, that is, of oneness, which bears the chain of continuous subjective and identitary transformation. Mathematically speaking, it is this *one* multiple subject or self that undergoes the processes of her or his transformability. Of course, this is no news to anyone, including the proponents of the theoretical project of the nonunitary subject. Therefore, what precludes the (feminist) poststructuralist language from uttering a word of this simple, self-evident fact, let alone theorizing its role in the construction of subjectivity?

There are two possible answers to this question that I am about to propose which are seemingly contradictory. Namely, the relevance of the "self-evident," "simple" fact is perceived as an implication of its irrelevance, precisely because of its self-evidence. This seemingly absurd claim and the situation it creates—of dim, unsaid, and peculiar inter-changeability in the two contradictory implications—are in full compliance with the logic of the discourse they pertain to, when they are seen in the context of their own conceptual world.

I will argue that the answer is already implicated in the preclusion itself. The poststructuralist feminist discourse seems to have assigned the status of the ineffable and the unthinkable to that "self-evident" instance of oneness or unity of the self or the "I" underlying the transformability of the subject. The very constitutive presuppositions of the school of thought in question create the implication that this is an instance outside the realms of language or outside the language at the disposal of this particular school of thought. Therefore, what seems to be implied is that this relevant instance is not so relevant after all.

In the position of "the one" there is a strikingly obvious coincidence with that of the real, issuing from the Lacanian psychoanalytic legacy that poststructuralism adheres to. Within the fringes of the Lacanian theoretical horizon, the real is interchangeable with both a substance and an instance. In one possible and clearly only approximate rendition of the point, let us say (resorting to ontological language) that the real is not an entity; it is a function. It is not a *quid*; it is a *quale*. It is a position that can be assumed by any-body or any-thing. It is a "status" that any-one and any-thing can assume for the other and for herself or himself.

Still, it seems that there is one "substance" which is always already assigned to assume the position of the real as its only possible positioning or rendition. Having the priority of residing only in and through the real, it is a substance that seems to be unquestionably exclusive to this topos; and this substance is the substance par excellence, the body or "the materiality."

The body—physicality or what is understood by "materiality"—in poststructuralist and (post-)Lacanian context is defined by its very inaccessibility to thought. It is equated with the real. It must be mediated through the Imaginary or via the language in order *to be there* for the subject. It is "impossibility" in the sense of its impossible immediacy. Inasmuch as it is "the bodily," it is the ineffable. It is beyond language and thought, and as such it is defined by its absence.

It seems that for poststructuralism, the notions of the real and the body as "materiality" are virtually synonymous. However, this is an oversimplification—and, to some degree, inaccurate—when the original writings and teachings of Lacan are taken into consideration; and we will return to this question in this book. Still, it appears that in the poststructuralist theory of gender identity, the interchangeability of the two concepts is in fact taking place. Moreover, it is taking the place of an axiom.

Anything produced by language—which is, in fact, anything not belonging to the domain of the "material"—is deemed to be radically and inexorably beyond the real. Or, it is the real, that "world of the impossible" or "impossible world," which remains to be conceived of as inaccessibly beyond the world of language. So, in the context of the poststructuralist theory of gender identity, it is inconceivable to thematize the real of an identity. The very predication would only be a *contradictio in adiecto*, the utterance itself but nonsense, since it is the radical detachment from the real that has created the Imaginary, the language, and, through that, the identity.

It is becoming ever more evident that the "outlandishness" of the real is generated by an underlying dichotomy of metaphysical origin nesting in the very foundations of the poststructuralist "production of worlds" (conceptual frameworks of explanatory practices). Clearly, the binary structure of opposition between "materiality" and the "idea" (= sign, culture), inherited through Marxism from the tradition of metaphysics, has subsisted as such even in the debates devoted to its deconstruction. This is another feature that the concept of "the one" and that of the real have in common. It is also captured in the binary structure of the classical metaphysical opposition and mutual exclusion of the one and the multiple, symmetrically coupling with the idea and matter.

As we saw above, besides the shared feature of being grasped in such a constitutive way by a dichotomy of a metaphysical character, the names of the one and the real have a few more traits in common that are of fundamental significance. These are the status of the ineffable, the status of the inaccessible, and, as I hope to demonstrate in the text, a constitutive intertwining with the concept of the body. (In *Bodies That Matter*, Judith Butler endeavors to overcome the mutually exclusivist interrelating between body and language, and this something I will be tackling in the next chapter.)

2.2.2

In *Psychic Life of Power* by Judith Butler,[18] I found one of the rare explicit references in poststructuralist feminist philosophy to a possible *site* of continuity for the subject; and in a later work by the same author, *Undoing Gender* from 2004, I found a reiterated unequivocal claim about the "tasks of persistence and survival" for the "I." In *Psychic Life of Power*, following Foucault's line of theorizing the notions of the subject, power, and discourse, and more specifically his conceptualizations of the "body" and the "soul" and their respective roles in the subject formation, Butler refers to the body as "*the* site" of subject's transformativity. When considered as a possible site of transformation, the body is referred to in its "materiality" or physicality, that is, in its aspects of the real. In that sense, this "site of transformations" is inescapably the same and one. Thus, what is clearly said is that the subject is never really identical to itself, and is always already a process; and what is implicated is that the "site" of transformability subsists as the same and one. Surely the imagined body as a territory of signification undergoes change. Nonetheless inasmuch as it is "the site" that Butler refers to, it is the body proper conceived in its opposition to the "soul" (both terms are provided by Foucault himself). Therefore, the body in this context is physicality and it is the real, detached from the workings of the Imaginary and the language; it is a passive *site*. After stating clearly that "for Foucault, this process of subjectivation takes place centrally through the body,"[19] Butler engages in a critical reading of Foucault's main idea, which aims at amending his theoretical position by way of introducing a psychoanalytic perspective to it. Or the other way around: "that criticism will entail re-emergence of a Foucauldian perspective *within* psychoanalysis."[20] The main goal of such a theoretical move is the introduction of greater emphasis on the subject's inherent dimension of ambiguity. And what is meant by that is that the "subject" (or "identity") as the imprisoning effect of the "soul, "insofar as [it is] totalizing,"[21] is, apart from being constraining, also an instance that has "formative or generative effects."[22] These formative, generative effects are the results of precisely "the prohibition and restriction" imposed by the constraints of soul producing the "frame" of "imprisonment." Imprisonment is but the *form* of subjectivity generated through those processes of restriction and discipline. The subject is the only possible active instance. It is an agency, and yet again it is that *passive* imprint of constraint and imprisonment. Hence, the claim about the subject's constitutive ambiguity. This theoretical move of Butler is enabled by her critical rethinking of the clear-cut dichotomy between body and soul in Foucault, which she aims to undermine, bypass, or surpass: "The transposition of the soul into an exterior and imprisoning frame for the body vacates, as it were, the interiority of the body, leaving that interiority as a malleable surface for the unilateral effects of disciplinary power."[23]

This quotation which speaks of the body-soul (interiority-exteriority) opposition is inherently related to her critical observation that Foucault, in particular in *Discipline and Punish*, reduces "soul" to the subject taken as a "position" within the Symbolic order, to use Lacanian parlance.[24] With this in mind, Butler says that Foucault's discourse on subjectivity, if not supplemented with psychoanalytic theory, leaves little space, if any, for the "location" of resistance of the subject.

Where does resistance to or in disciplinary subject formation take place? Does the reduction of the psychoanalytically rich notion of psyche to that of the imprisoning soul eliminate the possibility of resistance to normalization and to subject formation, a resistance that emerges precisely from the incommensurability between psyche and subject?[25]

Butler rejects recourse to the "romanticized" notion of the unconscious as a possible answer (proposed by psychoanalysis) to the question of the location of resistance (*for* the subject): "What makes us think that the unconscious is any less structured by the power relations that pervade cultural signifiers than is the language of the subject?"[26] She attempts to transport the ambiguity that marks the Foucauldian subject—its two-faceted, passive-active character ensuing from the subject's "complicity" with the power in the disciplinary formation—into the unconscious. The result of such a gesture is, however, not fruitful. Namely, it becomes even more difficult to establish the location and trace the mechanisms of resistance within the psyche. It is at this point, a virtual dead end in the discussion, that Butler reintroduces the question of the "body": "Before continuing this interrogation of psychoanalysis, however, let us return to the problem of the bodies in Foucault."[27] By searching for that which is outside the Foucauldian "soul," outside the subject articulated by the mechanisms of power—that mere "position" within the Lacanian Symbolic—as the possible *locus of resistance* (for the "I"), Butler is attempting to locate that thing which "glues the bundle [called subject] together." How do I come to such a conclusion? To answer this question let us consider the following hypothesis.

If while one is searching for that topos of critique (regarding one's own subject-position) one finds oneself drawn into and taken by that transformative instance (which is a process), one remains inside the confines of a construct that is substitutable (for other identity and subject constructs). The locus of resistance is, however, a potentiality of situating oneself with a stance of critical detachment from the continuous autogenerated processes of subjection (of "being a subject"). Thus, it is a situating beyond the instance of transformability (which, by definition, belongs to the domain of the subject). It is an instance that continues to be there as a possibility of critical distance (or of a critical stance) with regard to the ceaseless processuality. In other words, this is a "location" of an always already possible critical positioning. It is the topos of emergence of *any* resistance to the oppressions effectuated through *any* subjectivity, and thus not taken by the power *structures* pertaining to the subject. This topos can only be that "thing" Braidotti calls the "glue" for the nonunitary subject. It is an instance of *continuity* and persistence (of the critical stance) beneath, behind, or beyond, or merely parallel to and detached from, the processes of subjection and identification.

The implicated link between resistance and continuity (of the "I") that I see in *Psychic Life of Power* is confirmed or affirmed by Butler herself in *Undoing Gender*, when she says "the possibility of my persistence as an 'I' depends upon my being able to do something with what is done with me."[28] *Undoing Gender* is a book that insists on the task of survival of the self. Still it "undoes" neither the concept of subjectivity as conceived in *Psychic Life of Power* nor the argument concerning the topology of the resistance and continuity as proposed in the same book. (The latter is explained further on.)

Can the body be the site of revolt?

Exploring the possibility of identifying the locus of resistance in Foucault (in particular in *Discipline and Punish*), whereby the "soul" or the "subject" have been dismissed as clearly named and claimed as "an instrument of power,"[29] Butler inevitably invests the core of her investigation in the direction of the issue of the "body" as that possible location (of resistance).

In this particular work of Michel Foucault, according to Butler's meticulous reading, the "subject" is nowhere to be read in the vein of its (the subject's, which is also power's) notorious ambivalence. This means that any possibility for the subject to also be interpreted as the bearer, location, or agency of resistance is already in advance dismissed; it is for this reason that she invites us to "return to the problem of bodies in Foucault."[30] This invitation is immediately followed by a question: "How and why is resistance denied to bodies produced through disciplinary regimes?"[31] This is an introduction to the subsequent brief investigation of the possibility of the "body," as conceptualized in Foucauldian discourse, being that sui generis topos of resistance. We read: "It appears there is an 'inside' to the body which exists before power's invasion. But given the radical exteriority of the soul, how are we to understand 'interiority' in Foucault? That interiority will not be a soul, and it will not be a psyche, but what will it be? Is this a space of pure malleability, one which is, as it were, ready to conform to the demands of socialization? Or is this interiority to be called, simply, the body? Has it come to the paradoxical point where Foucault wants to claim that the soul is the exterior form, and the body interior space?"[32]

If the answers to these questions were to be affirmative, we would be facing a rather conservative position by Foucault. And it would indeed be so, not only because such a statement would bear the anachronistic overtones of the traditional metaphysical contempt for the body, but also because it would leave *no space for a potentiality of resistance and critique*. Following Butler, I would also dismiss, already in advance, such a hypothetical reading, since it is in utter disagreement with the most fundamental presuppositions and concerns of the Foucauldian discourse: his statement about the soul's imprisoning effects on the body is a sufficient reason for such dismissal. In addition to this, let us mention that the concept of the "soul" in the context of the entire Foucauldian discourse is also, of course, neither reduced nor reducible to imprisonment and constraint: it is in addition the instance of liberation and pleasure, and subject to the advocated practices of self-cultivation (*souci de soi*) in volume 3 of *The History of Sexuality*, *The Care of the Self*.[33] My insisting—following Butler's insisting which is of the same kind we find in *Psychic Life of Power*—on such textual renditions that might resonate with overtones of conservatism is merely for the purposes of demonstrating the complexity, multidimensionality, and the instances of impasse in Foucault's writing.

Butler continues with her investigation of the possibility of the body being that site of revolt par excellence: "This 'subjection' or *assujetisse-ment* is not only subordination but a securing and maintaining, a putting into place of a subject, a subjectivation. The 'soul brings [the prisoner] to existence'; not unlike in Aristotle, the soul, as an instrument of power, forms and frames the body, stamps it, and in stamping it, brings it into being. In this formulation, there is no body outside of power, for the materiality of the body—indeed, materiality itself—is produced by and in direct relation to the investment of power."[34] These lines show clearly that, according to this particular discourse, power and the subject are merely synonymous, whereas the subject is *also* to be understood as the constraining soul effect, the imprisoning imprint on and grasp of the body. The search for any grounds of any pertinent assumption that the body (in its immanence) might represent that locus of insubordination and revolt turns out to be futile. It is futile because the body is not outside the reach of power and should be understood as the "material" resonance of the power structure pertaining to the disciplining soul.

The logic of Butler's argument is obvious: resistance should be located outside the subject and the power (inhabiting the subject); since it is proven that even the body is invaded by the power and discursiveness (structuring the subject), resistance is not to be found there (in the body) either. Further on in the same chapter of *Psychic Life of Power*,[35] Butler engages in a critical reading of the sparse account of resistance that Foucault offers in volume 1 of *The History of Sexuality*, *The Will to Knowledge*,[36] where he clearly states that there can be "no single locus of great Refusal, no soul of Revolt." Instead, one can talk of "multiple possibilities of resistance enabled by power itself."[37] This ambivalence of power that is at the same time the disciplinary and constraining force of the law *and* the very potentiality of resistance instills both of these facets in the subject, producing it as that same ambivalence. The process is "reconstructed" by Butler as follows: "For power in Foucault not only consists in the reiterated elaboration of norms or interpellating demands, but is formative or productive, malleable, multiple, proliferative, and conflictual. Moreover, in its resignifications, the law itself is transmuted into that which opposes and exceeds its original purposes. In this sense, disciplinary discourse does not unilaterally constitute a subject in Foucault, or rather, if it does, it *simultaneously* constitutes the condition for the subject's de-constitution."[38] This reading of the law's possibility of "transgressing" itself by means of its ceaseless reiterations is Butler's own reappropriation or reinvention of Foucault's theory and is the product of her methodological innovation, which consists in interconnecting Foucault's thought and Lacanian psychoanalysis. The "conflictual" nature is brought to the Butlerian subject by way of the relentless resignifications of the law, which is always the same. The parallel to the disciplining force of Power is found in Lacan's law.[39]

Let us carefully read the passage from the first volume of Foucault's *History of Sexuality*, which is the departure point of Butler's thesis about "the law's autotransgression": "there is no single locus of great Refusal, no soul of revolt, source of all rebellions, or pure law of the revolutionary. Instead there is a plurality of resistances, each of them a special case: resistances that are possible, necessary, improbable; others that are spontaneous, savage, solitary, concerted, rampant, or violent; still others that are quick to compromise, interested or sacrificial; by definition, they can only exist in the strategic field of power relations. But this does not mean that they are only a reaction or rebound, forming with respect to the basic domination an underside that is in the end always passive, doomed to perpetual defeat."[40]

It seems to me that Foucault's explication about the multiple workings of the resistance(s) is valid on the level of the social, that wider network of power relations. Furthermore, in this sense, it has no real bearing on the question of the *construction* of the subject and its inner organization, in particular with respect to its double potentiality of power. When referring to "individual resistances," Foucault is rather vague regarding the question of the "location" of that "odd term in relations of power"[41] which is resistance. He speaks of "focuses of resistance . . . inflaming certain points of the body, certain moments in life, certain types of behaviour."[42] The fact that the subject is constituted by power does not explain anything about how the law and resistance organize themselves within that *construction* called subject.

If we are to understand the subject as the instance of a sort of self-articulation of the power (or its articulation within the self), regularization of what might be the anarchic flux of those *quasi*-libidinal forces of power, we can presume the existence of that double nature of power on the level of the subject. This, however, is not the subject we meet in *Discipline and Punish*, at least not according to Butler's reading. Nevertheless, considering the ambivalent nature of power, and the ambivalence of the subject as being both an agency (of power) and a product of subjection, let us assume that, in any of Foucault's works, the subject's disciplinary nature is to be understood as always already permeable. Consequently, should we presume that the lacunae in the subject's disciplinary "nature" are the *loci* or the substance of resistance and revolt?

At this point, we are facing the immediacy of the question of how this other facet of power's double nature is articulated on the level of the subject. This is a question of location and structure, but also, and even more so, of conceptual content. In other words, what does the concept of resistance in Judith Butler's subject consist in? What is the subject's capacity of resistance "made of"? What concept constitutes it? Or, what is its name? Power is the "substance" of both the subject's discipline and resistance; and what we are searching for is that instance which can transform power from the oppressiveness of discipline into a force of revolt. That instance is also the critical stance, and we are in a search of the "location" and the conceptual content it is made of.

Having rejected the psychoanalytic concept of the unconscious as the location and content of resistance as "romantic,"[43] Butler in her appropriation and combination of both the Foucauldian and the psychoanalytic theory of subjectivity offers no counterproposal. Although

Butler has declared power to be the carrier and the origin of resistance, she does not profess a conceptualization of how power is transformed from disciplinary effect to revolutionary force. In *Undoing Gender*, which engages with the questions of subject's (self's) "survival" and "persistence," we also do not find an answer to the question about the mechanisms, content, and topology of this transformation. The only thing we meet regarding this issue is a reiteration of the statement about the ambiguous nature of power or norms.[44]

In effect, Butler's (and Foucault's) theory fails to provide a clear response to this question. Subjectivity remains to be explicitly formulated as a disciplinary instance, and is only implicitly understood as the agency of resistance. It is proclaimed by both Foucault and Butler as such—the agency of resistance and critique—on the basis of the implications provided by the presence of power as its constituent. Therefore, one concludes: the "location" of revolt has to be looked for elsewhere and outside of what is strictly known as "the subject." Furthermore, this "location" has to be the site of resistance for or within a certain self or an "I."

Since the revolt or resistance is that which enables the subject's self-critique and self-transformation, one is obliged to assume that there is a certain *continuity* of an "I" behind these transformations. After all, if a subject can "die" for a new one to be "born," one has to imagine a "territory" or a "period" of absence or lack, a fissure in the endless positive processes of change; certainly, if one assumes that the dissolution of the subject is lived, experienced, appropriated as one's own subject-dissolution, or death. If the extinguishing, the disappearance, of the subject is an experience of a self-dissolution, there is an instance that undergoes this experience and claims it as its own: it is "I" who is dying as the "I" I knew. It is the instance of continuity behind the changes, which claims possession of these changes as its own.

Moreover, in the context of Butler's (Foucauldian) theory, this instance of continuity is to be presumed to be the location of resistance, because it is from the standpoint of only that instance that one can introduce, undergo, and endure subjectivity transformations.

Connecting Continuity with Unity (in the Sense of Perseverance of Oneness)

How can we situate the idea of the self's continuity within the poststructuralist theory of gender, which professes the multiple and transformative subject? What is the position it can assume without establishing a conflict with and undermining the fundamental presuppositions of the discourse? At first glance, the notion of continuity seems to introduce an unavoidable conflict with the main stakes of the discourse in question. This is a discourse of consistent and relentless critique of the metaphysical, and the idea of continuity echoes with overtones of the eternal, stable, and fixed. These echoes are the product of the problematic implication about a relatively stable instance behind the processes of vicissitude and change. The stable instance bears a resemblance to unchangeable substance. Thus, it seems to imply an essence, a human essence universally shared by that multitude of posthumanist subjectivity. But if we are to understand that instance of continuity not as a substance, but as a stance, I cannot see the reason for any "conflict of discourses." In the context of poststructuralist discourse(s), there are a number of (in)stances that are perpetually there, such as the subject, the real, power, and so on, displaying that mere faculty of continuity within the discourse itself and the imagined reality it creates (a noneternal one, not representing an essence, but mutational and staggering—and yet, an instance of continuity).

The instance of continuity in its immanence functions as a unifying force for the self or the subjective processuality. In other words, continuity is the perseverance of a certain numeric one. Moreover, this enduring one underlies or undergoes the processes of indentificational multiplicity and subjective transformability. In the Foucauldian context, the instance of continuity and perseverance seems to have been assumed by a "substance," that continuous numeric unity of the *body* which participates in the processes of subjection as that which is exterior to language.

It is significant that Butler raises the question of the body as a possible site of the resistance, concluding that such a possibility is precluded or hindered by Foucault's discourse. Nonetheless, she embarks on an investigation into the reasons for these hindrances, and with that she seems to demonstrate her initial presumption that the body should be the right place to look for the possible location of resistance. In *Psychic Life of Power*, Butler opens this line of investigation with the following question: "let us return to the problem of bodies in Foucault. How and why is resistance denied to bodies produced through disciplinary regimes?"[45] What inspires Butler to pose this particular question? Is it the fact that what is being disciplined is the body and that thus it is the body which is called to its own resistance to whatever subjugates it? Foucault remarks that "the dissociated Self"—the one "adopting the illusion of a substantial unity"—is possible precisely through the destruction of the body, that "volume in perpetual disintegration" (inflicted by language and ideas).[46] So, it seems that Butler expects the body to resist this "force of destruction," to strive necessarily for its self-preservation, for its survival, for its continuity. This also implies that the body is the instance which has the inherent capacity for and immanent tendency toward continuity; it is precisely this characteristic which provides the basis for the expectation that the site par excellence of the resistance should be the body. Thus, we can deduce, following this line of reasoning, that there is an instance of continuity for the "I" provided by the incessant effort of the body to preserve itself against the disintegration brought about and upon it by the subject.

From the discussion thus far, we can see that, through the presumed corporeal continuity, Butler provides a potentiality to conceive of a certain continuity for the "I," marked by transformative subjectivity.

Also, let us add the following observation: in spite of the fragmentations brought about by the many subject deaths that an "I" undergoes, some continuity for the subject is also assumed in the sense of the continuity of the memory line of experiences (unless we are speaking of psychotic subjects). This continuity of the memory unifies the many subject-situations under a single name. In both Butler's and Foucault's writings, it is appears to be an "epistemological given" that this interrupted sequence of subjectivities is located within a circumscribed psychic "space" as a single unit or set.

Evidently, in the discourses purporting the "death of the unitary subject," the workings of self-sustainability of the "one" next to the "multiple" are always already tacitly admitted, but never clearly referred to. The silence imposed over the "Name of the One" is in inherent, inextricable relation with the "prohibition" of the use of language regarding the questions of continuity. One can assume operations of a self-imposed, ideological control over the "good" and "bad" words in the context of these particular discourses: words to be subject to repetition and words to be avoided.

The silently admitted instance of continuity in the discourses of the nonunitary subject, transformed into a stance of speech or text, could allow the opening of spaces for discussion, linguistic possibilities for thematizing questions of forms and instances of unity for the subject in process.

The Radical Solitude in Continuity

"Many people think that grief is privatizing, that it returns us to a solitary situation, but I think it exposes the constitutive sociality of the self, a basis of thinking a political community of a complex order," writes Judith Butler in one of her later works.[47] And I concur with her position. Grief is a state of being exposed in one's constitutive dependence on others, since "the ties we have to the others"[48] indeed "compose who we are."[49] Still, those "many people" who "think that grief is privatizing" are probably also right, since the grieving, or rather, the mourning, entails the hard labor of self-preservation performed by the "I" in the face of the dread of its possible annihilation.

The relentless, autogenerated process of corporeal and psychic self-preservation against the threat of disintegration by "the dissociated Self" is a state of irrevocable solitude. This is a process of repetition of the single labor of autopropagation, of ceaseless repetition of an act of unilateral autoaffirmation. I am resorting to the term "unilateral" in its Deleuzian sense of "unilateral difference,"[50] which is a singular, unrelated act of affirmation, of a "sheer yes." The "sheer yes" of the survival is always already an autoreferential affirmation doomed to endless repetition.

The autoreferential stance is always already translating itself into an autoreflexive one.[51] We are speaking of an autoaffirmative process of self-preservation striving toward the continuity of that particular "auto-." This ceaseless duration of self-preserving labor takes the figure of curving of the self into itself, similar to the Nietzschean idea of the self's will that turns upon and against itself as the origin and perpetual act of autoreflexivity and, hence, subjectivity.[52]

And this is a state of insurmountable, radical solitude. The question whether it is prior to, posterior to, or contemporaneous with the "entrance on the scene" of the other is, in fact, irrelevant. When it is relative or viewed as denuded of any relation, there is an instance of radical solitude in the self involved in the autogenerating and autoreflexive processes of subject production. In other words, behind, beneath, or parallel to the mobility of the multiple and transformable subject, the hard labor of self-preserving continuity is taking place, creating a state that is an irrevocably solitary one.

This is a self-enclosed reality of mere labor at a point where the organic and the sense of selfhood merge into each other, a denuded effort of self-preservation that is ultimately elusive to the authority of language. It is the instance of the unsurpassable "imprisonment" in one's own self. This instance is the real of the "I" that is unmediated through the other and through language. This irrevocably *solitary* instance delineates the limits of automediation through the other. It introduces the limit to the reach of language.

2

ON THE REAL AND THE IMAGINED

THE DICHOTOMY OF SEX AND GENDER AND SOME OF ITS "METAPHYSICAL" IMPLICATIONS

The dichotomy of "sex" and "gender" and the still prevailing ways in which it works within the contemporary theories of gender are the reflection, or rather, the expression, of another dichotomy that belongs to the family of several grand couples of opposing concepts inherited from the metaphysical tradition. Poststructuralist theories of gender from the last decades of the twentieth century and the beginning of the twenty-first perpetuate the classical metaphysical binaries in spite of the consensually shared goal of transcending or doing away with metaphysics altogether. Postmodernism's method of surpassing metaphysical thinking has consisted in the philosophical decision of not tackling what is probably the central classical dichotomy of metaphysics—that between the "real" and the "unreal" as the inaccurate mental representation of the real. Such a priori refusal to pose the question of the real speaks to what Quentin Meillassoux terms a "correlationist" axiom of thought. Meillassoux's concept of correlationism refers to the post-Kantian legacy of thought that always already forecloses the possibility of thinking the real.

Adhering to the Kantian prohibition on penetrating the real by thought is not a remnant of metaphysics per se. The philosophical decision, however, to affirm the "unreal" or the mentally produced reality as the only possible reality is grounded in metaphysics. Namely, it is a choice in favor of one of the opposing terms in a couple, but the couple itself is metaphysically construed. Arguing that fiction is the only reality available to us is arguing in favor of a term that is constituted by its opposition to the metaphysical real, a term whose meaning is conditioned by its status in a metaphysically construed binary.

The dichotomy between sex and gender reflects and reproduces the opposition between the real and the unreal. It also represents the classical metaphysical division between "materiality" (of the body and sex) and the "idea" (or "the linguistic character" of gender). It seems that the oldest philosophical opposition, which is at the same time the founding metaphysical binary, generates a series of other inherently related binaries based on mutual exclusion and opposition of their constituting terms. Namely, the opposition of biology and culture or materiality and idea inevitably comes down to the dichotomy of reality (the real) and fiction. This radical dichotomy, which does not necessarily have to be philosophical, has always already been transposed into the binary of *tò ón* (the Being) and *tò mē on* (the non-Being or nothingness) in Western philosophy.

In *Bodies That Matter* Judith Butler exposes the naïve, or the naïvely unquestioned, belief in the existence of a "pure body," thereby stabilizing the binary between materiality or biology and discursivity or cultural constructedness.[1] The belief in the "pure body" that is detached from language in a defining way is but a belief in the absolutely passive body. Or rather, it is a belief in the absolute passivity of *matter* and *matter* as absolute passivity, on the one hand, and the untouched sovereignty of subject's intentionality, on the other.

In discourses created by this traditional dichotomy, the subject's intentionality obtains a position that is traditionally categorized as the "self" and transcendentally developed into a universe referred to as "I," from which it is expected to ontologically operate independently from the body. Thus, it can operate on the body as form on matter, as intentionality on material, as subject on object. In other words, let us say, paraphrasing Judith Butler, that what we are dealing with here is the classical dichotomy between determinism (= materiality of sex) and (subject's) free will inventing gender.[2]

Such trenchant and stable opposition between sex and gender, and thus between the body and the construction of subjectivity and identity (materiality and "the world of ideas"), is made possible and persists precisely through the dichotomy between reality (real) and fiction (the imagined). This particular dichotomy inevitably creates a significant implication that seems to (auto)undermine some of the basic assertions of poststructuralist theory itself. The implication at stake is that "matter" is "certainty" because it will always remain outside the limits of language. One the other hand, language as an instance of incessant transformation, subject to history and, therefore, contingency, will remain on the other side or on "this side," that is, the only accessible side of the unyielding and nonpenetrable frontier of the inconceivable "real."

This mode of reasoning based on the mutual exclusion and opposition of the two terms necessarily implies that the real is "more real" than fiction (or the Imaginary). This claim is obviously tautology. Yet, it seems that the correlationists, the poststructuralists, and the postmodernists claim the opposite. The absurd is sublimated into a paradox. The paradox is grounded in the dichotomy, even when the claim is that there is no reality except the only reality available to us. Even when the real is annulled, the annulment is enabled by the presupposition that the Imaginary or language or fiction cancels the reality of the opposing term. The very binary nonetheless intimates that there is "real reality" (even though it is "unavailable" to the thinking subject) which is opposed to the imagined reality (the only one available to us). Therefore, in the context of the binary at issue, the real acquires the status of a "higher reality," in spite of its unthinkability and inaccessibility and its being rendered impossible.

It is precisely the axiomatic position of the assumption about the opposition of reality and fiction—and the need for ontological certainty that it satisfies—which makes possible both (a) the conservative or "metaphysically inspired" resistance to the discourses of constructivism and (b) constructivism's own reluctance regarding the possibility of deconstructing the concepts of "materiality" and "sex." From a constructivist, just as from a nonconstructivist, point of view, sex as materiality cannot be subject to deconstruction, since it is precisely the opposite of construction—nature and matter. It is precisely this classical constructivist position that has served Judith Butler as a point of departure in her critical exposure of the incongruity at the heart of the constructivist argument. The incongruity in question sustains and reinforces the dichotomous and oppositional interpositioning of "sex" and "gender": "If such a theory [of 'the radical constructivist position'] cannot take account of sex as the site or surface on which it acts, then it ends up presuming sex as the unconstructed, and so concedes the limits of linguistic constructivism, inadvertently circumscribing that which remains unaccountable within the terms of construction."[3] Let us engage in a closer reading of Butler's deconstruction of the materiality of the body and of the culturality or constructedness of gender as well as the opposition they create. Our reading will aim to identify the symptoms of presence of the dichotomy of the real and fiction and its effects, and also investigate the modes in which it operates and the implications it generates.

I will argue that the aporetic situation with respect to reality (the real) in which the construction of sex finds itself at one point in the text of *Bodies That Matter* is symptomatic of the dichotomy of the real and fiction inherent in Butler's discourse too, just as it is in those who are subject to her critique. At one point in Butler's argumentation, one encounters a productively paradoxical position in the category of reality that screens the crisis of the perennial dichotomy between the real and fiction. She brings the discussion to the wall of aporia by exposing the dead end of this conflict of duality of concepts in such a denuding way that the binary is necessarily subverted. Notwithstanding the subversion, the radical critique that unveils the ambivalent, paradoxical ways in which both terms operate and interchange, the binary itself continues to be there, always already presupposed.

Butler's critique of the theoretical propagation of the opposition between sex and gender as one that is between materiality and construction and that relies on the belief in the cultural "virginity" of the body sets out with an aphoristic remark: "is sex to gender as feminine is to masculine?"[4] Butler encapsulates many important aspects of her critique in this allusion to the structuralist opposition of the female and male gender as a reflection of that between nature and culture.[5] Nonetheless, I will resort to this remark only in order to rephrase it in the following way: "Is sex to gender as nature is to culture?"; and thereof, "Is sex to gender as reality is to fiction?" The latter is the question I would like to concentrate on in this chapter of the book.

Let us reiterate: the binary of reality and fiction is among the several grand and grounding dichotomies of all metaphysics. In other words, it represents the theme that has always already been at the base (or at the pinnacle) of any and all metaphysical endeavors: the problem of the real and the illusion that always already "translates" and transposes itself into the problem of truth and delusion.[6]

In short, the question of the dichotomy of the real and fiction has always already been or has inevitably imposed or transposed itself as the question of "what is" and "what is not"—the question of *tò ón* and *tòmē on*, of Being and non-Being.

THE IMPASSES OF THE DUALITY OF THE REAL AND FICTION: THE "APORETIQUE(S)"

Already at the very beginning of the critical endeavor undertaken in *Bodies that Matter*, namely, to deconstruct the dual structure of sex and gender, one senses an anticipation of a fruitful theoretical outcome: a radical rethinking of both concepts and their interrelatedness. The deconstructive critical reading carried out by Butler in this work brings forth the liberation of both terms from the hold of the (binary) structure, and from their oppositional and mutually exclusive relation. The joy from such anticipation may, however, be a little disquieted by the inhibiting situation in which, at certain point in the argumentation, the notion of sex *as construction* finds itself in relation to the term of reality. We read:

> If gender is the social construction of sex, and if there is no access to this "sex" except by means of its construction, then it appears not only that sex is absorbed by gender, but that "sex" becomes something like a fiction, perhaps a fantasy, retroactively installed at a prelinguistic site to which there is no direct access. But is it right to claim that "sex" vanishes altogether, that it is *a fiction over and against what is true*, that it is *a fantasy over and against what is reality*? Or do these very oppositions need to be rethought such that *if "sex" is a fiction, it is one within whose necessities we live, without which life itself would be unthinkable*? *And if "sex" is a fantasy, is it perhaps a phantasmatic field that constitutes the very terrain of cultural intelligibility*? Would such a rethinking of such conventional oppositions entail a rethinking of "constructivism" in its usual sense?[7]

As I read this paragraph, Butler seems to claim that sex does not disappear entirely by virtue of being that "fiction" within whose "necessities we live," and without which "life itself would be unthinkable." This seems to be Butler's answer to her own implied presupposition that the fiction or fantasy is something which, by definition, is to be expected to inevitably establish a relation of opposition to "what is true" and to "reality." I detect this presupposition in the very possibility of the question of whether it is right to claim that "sex," conceived as radically constructed, "vanishes altogether," that it is a "fiction over and against what is true and reality." We are immediately compelled to ask how this "necessary" fiction relates to that which she refers to as "true" and "reality." In other words, the argument that the fiction of sex functions as the real even though it is not the real intimates that there is a real which is more real than this fiction. It intimates that Butler's conceptualization of the fiction (of sex) is grounded in oppositional thinking in terms of the classical binary of the real and fiction (or the Imaginary or the conceptual) establish.

Furthermore, I need to pose the question of what is "true" and what is "reality" according to the core argument in *Bodies That Matter*. Clearly, Butler distinguishes the categories of "true" and "reality" from that of "fiction." She also posits the two categories as distinct from each other, while at the same time treating them as interchangeable ("a fiction over and against what is true, that it is a fantasy over and against what is reality?"). The "phantasmatic field" of the body constitutes a reality, that of "cultural intelligibility." The fact that it has to be affirmed as a reality of a sort betrays a binary logic according to which fiction and the real establish two opposing terms. It appears that there is a "more real" reality than that established by the phantasmatic field (that the body is), and that Butler attempts to rethink the relation between the two. Consequently and inevitably, we are also led to the questions of what and where we should assume this "real reality" is. Is it perhaps that "prelinguistic site to which there is no direct access"? If the answer to this question turns out to be affirmative, it would generate a series of rather interesting implications about the main concerns and claims in Butler's theory that she shares with the rest of the poststructuralist theories on gender and identity.

It seems to me that Butler is suggesting that the very status of necessity (*ananke, Zwang*) that the fiction of "sex" (and its "materiality") holds constitutes an aspect, a component, a situation, or a part of a topology of the only possible reality we can encounter, be in, live, or think—that of the language. The "fiction of sex" *performs* (as) the "reality of sex." It possesses the authority of an undisputable criterion of ultimate formative power in the production of the gendered and sexualized identities and possibilities of practice; and the identities and practices that defy this defining criterion and foundation are determined in the last instance by that very defiance. Following the logic of Butler's argumentation, I am led to conclude that the "fiction of sex" *is* the "reality of sex" (the reality that genders are bound to relate to). Fiction is reality, the only reality to be found out there.

Could this be the solution to the aporia created by the encounter of the constructivist concept of sex (as fiction) with the notion of reality? It is possible. Or rather, it would be possible only if this were a statement situated outside a discourse based on a binary mode of thinking and constituted around and by a dualistic structure. In fact, it would be a possible way out of the aporia only if this statement were not produced within a discourse created by a duality (albeit deconstructed) and the interconditioning interrelatedness (albeit deconstructed) of the two terms.

The ambivalence of terms enclosed in a binary relation can hardly be "a productive paradox" in the sense of productivity that we are in search of here—thought that enables a way out of the aporetic vicious circles of philosophy. Instead, the only thing that this paradox can produce is a circular entrapment between the two poles of the binary. Such vicious circularity is the necessary product of a binary in which the two terms are opposed and mutually exclusive. Mutual exclusion, I will argue, is always already produced by a binary structure of thinking, by any dual construct.

Let us subject what I will call the map of symptoms of the quoted paragraph by Butler to a radical, critical reading in an attempt to unveil a tradition of thought about the real and reality, which is determined in its last instance by what François Laruelle calls "philosophical sufficiency" (as explained in the previous chapter). According to Laruelle, this opposition has always already persisted in a form of thought he identifies as "gréco-judaïque," philosophy.[8] This is not a claim about the superiority of Western philosophy. Quite the contrary, it is an argument about the radical historicity of the mode of thinking called philosophy. Certainly, there exist Eastern philosophies. But would they identify themselves as philosophy in the essentially European sense in which we understand this word? Did the West include them in the "universal" history of philosophy through a procedure of approximation with its own model of thinking determined as "philosophy"?[9]

The opposition between the real and fiction has never ceased to be the fundament of philosophy, insists Laruelle. This fact remains unchanged even in the texts belonging to the philosophical project of deconstruction of the Heideggerian (and Derridean) line of thinking.[10] The proclaimed Western metaphysical philosophical thought and the self-proclaimed postmetaphysical philosophical thought belong to the same tradition of thought. The pillar of this tradition is the opposition between the real and fiction. It is the defining trait of all Western ("gréco-judaïque") philosophy, rendering it in its entirety, including deconstruction and Lacanian psychoanalysis, metaphysical,[11] argues Laruelle.

TWO WAYS OF DEALING WITH AN APORETIC DEAD END: DELEUZE AND LARUELLE

I would like to consider two concepts, one central for a philosophical line of thinking and the other for the non-philosophical striving to create an opening for thought that escapes the binary clench. Deleuze proposes a way out of the confinement of thought within a stable structure and, consequently, out of the binary of opposites that is the most elemental compulsory constituent of any structure. Laruelle too proposes a thesis about an exit from dualism. Moreover, Laruelle's exiting dualism means exiting philosophy altogether. The exit from the dual autoenclosure of thought is enabled by the non-philosophical method of "thinking in terms of the real." I will discuss and compare Deleuze's and Laruelle's proposals; the need to compare them stems from one central element they have in common—the goal to produce theorizing that is determined by immanence.

Let us start with Deleuze. The dissolution of structure into a rhizomatic flux produces liberating effects with respect to stability and exclusionism as the necessary and defining aspects of structure. However, it disables the possibility of thinking "the pure concepts," that is, concepts seen in their aspect of what Deleuze calls "unilateral difference."[12] Dissolution not only of structure but also of concepts as such is at the core of Deleuze's "cosmology," especially in his early works. His ontology and epistemology of dissolution are already implied in the conceptualization of "unilateral difference" in *Différence et répétition* from 1968. Unilateral difference is an unequivocal "yes" (of "Being"): an unrelated and absolute (act of) affirmation. It produces a flux of "will" (in the parlance of Nietzsche, whose formative influence on his own work is claimed by Deleuze himself) or of "being" (in classical philosophical terms) or of "energy" (in terms Deleuze uses later), instead of a definitive and defining structure.

Dissolution of structure is what Deleuze pursues, together with Guattari, also in *L'Anti-Oedipe* (*Anti-Oedipus*)[13] and *Mille Plateaux* (*A Thousand Plateaus*).[14] In these two works, structure is dismantled, dissolving into rhizomes of traces and fluctuation, into bodies without organs.

The dissolution of concepts themselves into either rhizomes (in *L'Anti-Oedipe*) or endless affirmations of absolute or unilateral differences (in *Différence et répétition*)[15] is what precludes the possibility of thinking "pure concepts." The very impossibility of isolating single concepts from the rhizomatic influxes created by dissolving concept-structures disables any attempt to think concepts unilaterally or in their singularity.

The impossibility at issue is the result of a *philosophical decision* in the Laruellian sense. It consists in a gesture of philosophical positing of a world or positing of a philosophical world. It is a gesture by which the real is substituted by the transcendental or by thought, and what makes it philosophical, according to Laruelle, is the "amphibology" between the two categories that is thereby instituted. Amphibology, as explained in chapter 1 and in the introduction, as the essence of all and any philosophy consists in the indiscernibility between the instances of the real and thought and the possibility of endless circular intersubstitution. The unstoppable movement of circularity is not marked by reciprocity but rather by radical asymmetry. The inferior term in this asymmetry is the real.

Deleuze's philosophical decision is one that cancels out in advance any theoretical attempt to think "pure concepts" since, within his philosophical cosmology, they are determined in the last instance as metaphysically stabilized truths. The only permitted critique of metaphysical certainty and stable, fixed truths is that which adds up to Deleuze's cosmology of fluxes and rhizomes. A Deleuzian solution to the aporia in question can be found in his philosophical metaphors of the "labyrinth" and the "eternal return" and the equation he establishes between them.

In *Nietzsche et la philosophie* from 1962, Deleuze explains that there is no way out of the labyrinth of aporias.[16] The only way out consists in embracing the truth about the unending circle of paradoxical thought. The image of the "labyrinth" we encounter in *Nietzsche et la philosophie* represents the Great Circle of the eternal return (*le retour éternel*).[17] The labyrinth is the figure of the Deleuzian and Nietzschean ontology of temporality as the nontemporality of the eternal return. (Deleuze's considerations about time and temporality, presented also in some of his other works,[18] follow the views of Bergson, according to whom time inasmuch as it is pure duration is only the future always already collapsing into the returning past. This vision conforms to the one of the eternal return.)

According to Deleuze, the affirmation of the labyrinth, the consistent philosophical observance of the *decision* not to leave it but rather to remain inside, brings about salvation from the aporia. Contrary to Deleuze, it is my conviction that the affirmation of the labyrinth does not resolve the problem of the aporia. Instead, it is its "unilateral affirmation" in ceaseless repetition. By affirming an aporetic situation, we might be resolving some sense of frustration created by it, but the aporia itself persists. We might be resolving our relation to it; but seen in its singularity, seen unilaterally, aporia remains untouched by our way of positioning with respect to it.

My central argument here is that the aporetic situation is possible only within a discourse of duality (or dualism) that implies opposition between two components of a founding binary structure, and that that constitutive contrariety issues in mutual exclusiveness. Consequently, a situation of thought outside of a sense of aporia should be an unavoidable sign, a certain symptom of *real*, *experienced*, or *lived* liberation from—and dissolution of—the binary constraint.

François Laruelle's choice in *Philosophie et non-philosophie* is to attempt to invent a mode of thinking that is outside the aporetic labyrinth, to confer a possibility of thinking in a nonaporetic situation. According to Laruelle's non-philosophy, an exit from aporia, is enabled only by thought in terms of the real (*la pensée du réel*). In fact, the very project of "non-philosophy," the idea about the necessity of a radical stepping out of philosophy and the assumption of a non-philosophical posture of thought, relies on precisely on the concept of a thought in the terms of the real. Namely, the suspension of the principle of philosophical sufficiency (*principe de philosophie suffisante*, or PPS)[19] is a gesture of thought that correlates with the real while it simultaneously affirms its ultimate evasion of language and thought. It is a kind of thinking that recognizes the uncompromising and uncontrollable rule of an ungraspable real behind the reality it aspires to explain. It affirms the ultimate authority of the real, which dictates the "generating of truths" and not scholastic axioms, including those of non-philosophy.

In that sense, the non-philosophical posture of thought is an empty position—a nonposition—within philosophy which makes use of this position as a sort of conceptual material (*chôra*),[20] which is ultimately heretical toward it and faithful only to the specificity and singularity of the theorized reality. Departing from such a presupposition, one should be able to think "real" and "fiction" each in their singularity, "in terms of their specificity," liberated from the interconditioning dependence on the other term (of the binary). Laruelle writes:

> The problem of philosophy in general originates from the fact that
> it never thinks of the terms in their specificity, but as contrary to

each other, within their relations, and, in the best case, on their borders and in their proximity. As a result of this, the concept of the real, like any other [concept], designates an amphibologic reality, a limitrophy of the real, regardless of whether it is placed beyond the real or before it or as a border between the two. From classical rationalism to contemporary deconstructions, fiction has remained captured within that relation of the mixed, that is, of the unitary. Excluded by the real, internalized by it, while internalizing it itself and pretending to codetermine it, [fiction] has never escaped these games of interinhibition, which are those that philosophy plays with itself, where it is but a pawn of a history which has pretended to surpass it.[21]

As explained in the first chapter, the notion of "unitary" in Laruelle refers to a philosophical gesture of unifying differences in a transcendental construct of conceptual interrelatedness. The interrelatedness is a totalizing unity of binaries and multiplicities resulting in an all-encompassing one, which could be a system or an antisystem. Nonetheless, it is a "cosmology," a philosophical universe, and it demands consistency with or fidelity to the principles of the doctrine even when it pretends to be an antisystem.

Interinhibition of the two terms is a relation that any binary ultimately produces. It is the inevitable result of the interconditioning relatedness of an opposing and conflicting kind. In the previous chapter, we explained how and why, according to Laruelle, thinking in terms of the real is also thinking in terms of the one. In order to avoid the paralyzing effects of aporia, in order to arrive at thought uninhibited by coupling, one has to radicalize it by using the "syntax of the real."[22] Thinking according to the syntax of the real is thinking in radical terms or that uses radical concepts. Concepts are radical only when they are transcendentally impoverished, which brings them to their determination in the last instance.[23]

WHERE DOES THE REALITY LIE?
FANTASIES OF THE LOCUS OF THE REAL

François Laruelle proposes the method—a posture of thought rather than a method in the strict sense of the word, that is, a specified procedure stipulated by a doctrine—of the Vision-in-One (*la Vision-en-Un*) as a way of thinking in terms of the singular, the absolute,[24] and the real.[25] This vision, this *theoria-en-heni*, emerges as radically free from any dually and, consequently, structurally conditioned mode of thinking. The Vision-in-One, in Laruelle's view, is the only axiomatic positioning of thought that enables an ultimately radical critique and a way out of not only metaphysics but the entire "gréco-judaïque" matrix of thought,[26] that is, Occidental philosophy. This is so because only thinking in terms of the one, argues Laruelle, can escape the trap of the "gréco-judaïque" obsession with the unitary thought of organizing differences in a unified and unifying whole as the central constituent of metaphysics.[27]

Oneness and radicalness in the sense of non-relatedness and immanence are the defining constituents of non-philosophical, that is, of nondichotomous, thinking. Unitary thought (*unitaire*, in the sense criticized by Laruelle) is *relational*. It is a posture of thought that establishes relations between different concepts by way of organizing them into a construct, an organic whole that is a unity of a multiplicity of concepts. The exclusion of the possibility of thinking outside the unity formed by a relation of at least two, according to Laruelle, is informed by the intentions characteristic of metaphysics and philosophy. Unitary (*unitaire*) thought is always already dualistic (*dualitaire*). On the other hand: "The one is an identity, which is *nonthetic* [*non-thétique*] in general, that is, nondecisional (of) itself and nonpositional (of) itself: without will for essence, without topology for existence."[28] The Vision-in-One is also an experience that is "nonreflected [irreflechie], nondecisional, and nonpositional (of itself); the one is an entirely singular immanence."[29]

In short, according to Laruelle, the reality examined by a thought that situates itself as correlating with the real emerges within a vision liberated from the unitary (dualistic) ambitions of thought, that is to say, outside the theoretical horizon of relationism. Hence, the thought in terms of the real is absolute in a very distinct sense: it is solitary in its singularity, an effort of thought exposed in its ultimate incapacity to grasp and control the rule of the real, yet attempting to correlate with it without the support of a doctrinal web made of philosophical decisions. The reality that is subject to thought in terms of the real is experiential, as well as initially and ultimately nonreflected (*irreflechie*). Nonetheless, thought correlating with the real ceaselessly subjects this reality to its theoretical vision (or Vision-in-One). It is singular; and such is the method of thinking in terms of the real or the Vision-in-One. Namely, it is a process of theorizing that recognizes itself in its last instance—or in its "identity in the last instance,"[30] in Laruellian parlance—as nonreflected, that is, as being inextricably grounded in the remainder of the elusive real, singular and severed from the network of philosophical decision(s).

Let us now go back to the paragraph quoted from Butler's *Bodies That Matter*. It concludes with the suggestion that "sex" represents such "fiction" within whose "necessities we live" and without which "life itself would be unthinkable." This is the answer she offers to the question of whether it is right "to claim that 'sex' vanishes altogether, that it is *a fiction over and against what is true*, that it is *a fantasy over and against what is reality*" (italics mine). If this were the ultimate implication of "radical constructivism," we would have to radically "rethink 'constructivism' in its usual sense," suggests Butler.

I would like to raise the question of the source of this dilemma. It is based on an implication—which acts as the grounding presupposition for the entire argument—about the opposition between reality and fiction. Butler does not attempt to deconstruct the opposition itself. Subject to her radical (deconstructive) critique is each of the terms, which exposes them in their constructedness and in their mutual relatedness.

However, the binary construct, and its logic of opposition in particular, escapes the process of deconstruction. Butler solves the dilemma of "fiction against reality"—and "what is true"—by redistributing new significations (and power) within the binary, not by deconstructing the binary itself. She simply shifts the asymmetry in favor of fiction.

According to Butler, it is a necessary fiction, one without which "life itself would be unthinkable." Even if it is "over and against what is true," even if "it is a fantasy over and against what is reality," its stipulating workings demand discursive recognition and legitimization precisely because the "weight" of its significance is that of an inescapable precondition of our existences. We are compelled to ask: if this "necessity without which life is unthinkable," that is, "the fiction of sex," remains opposed to or radically different from "the reality," where and what then is "the reality" and where and what is "the true"?

If we are to suppose that the reality is somewhere outside the realm of our immediate experience—which is, nonetheless, one of mediation, that is, of fiction as life constituting necessity—and outside the borders of the reality that is the only one thinkable and possible to us, where should we assume the topos of that "real reality" is? Where and what could this topos of "reality," and of "the true" as opposed to fiction, possibly be? The notion of fiction in this context is synonymous with the Lacanian notion of the Imaginary and, consequently, it implies the production of the Symbolic. It is, therefore, as professed precisely by the poststructuralists, the only reality available to us. Yet, Butler speaks of the possibility for the reality of fiction or fantasy to be over and against "reality" and "what is true." If the reality is outside the only reality we can think (of), constitute, and be constituted by, namely, that of the "necessary fiction," then where and when (and as what) are we expecting it to be "located"?

By posing and presupposing such questions, it would seem, one assumes the existence of a reality parallel to the only reality we can experience as such, that is, a counterreality. Are we, by this, supposing the existence of a reality that is "more real" than the one we are experiencing immediately? If that is so, the immediately experienced reality will be our (mis)conception of "the real reality." The latter, on the other hand, will assume the status of a more perfect reality (than the one mentally construed). In fact it will assume the status of the perfect reality, the absolute. Once again, the "out there" will receive the status of the absolute, of "the more real" than the reality subject to human experience. At the same time, "the more real" is equated with "the more true." It is beyond the reach of human experience and it is perfect. It is transcendental reality or the transcendental substitution of the reality. We do not speak of the positive reality of the transcendental activity, but of the subterfuge of the transcendental in place of the real. It is an abstraction, a pure concept, that has been granted ontological independence on the basis of a philosophical decision. Evidently, we are facing the perennial metaphysical aporia, present since the time of Parmenides.

Thus to which reality could the construction of sex (or of gender or any other of the constructions according to which "we are living as according to the very necessities of our lives") possibly be contrary? If by reality the "impossible real" of psychoanalysis is not meant, then, it seems, we are dealing with yet another discursive construction. If the impossible real is seen as "more real" than the construction to which it is opposed, then we would be dealing with a more perfect reality and one of greater correspondence with the real itself (psychoanalytic or not), yet one that is another abstraction, a conceptual construct. This would be then a theological thesis.

Butler's notion of the real is a Lacanian one. Throughout all of her work, she has explicitly adopted and operated with Lacan's concept of the Real as the unthinkable and the impossible site of existence. The real has to be mediated via language, and it is only the realm of language and the topologies of discourse that the human subject can inhabit. It is beyond the "liveable life" that is always already created by the Imaginary and structured as the Symbolic, if we put it in Lacanian terms. The real has its absurd effect on life that is unintelligible as such

and only experienced as the uncanny. Unless re-created by the mediation of the Imaginary and instituted in the world (in the Laruellian
sense) through the Symbolic, unless translated into a "meaning," into
an instance of the language, it virtually does not exist for the subject.
The subject is a purely linguistic category.

Yet, it appears that in the above quoted paragraph by Butler, and, for
that matter, in the entire analysis laid out in *Bodies That Matter*, it is the
proximity to the real of a certain imaginarily constructed reality that
renders it "more real" than the one closer to the fantasy. Although sex is
a construct (as she demonstrates in the book), it also opposes a certain
remainder within it which is "more real." Could that be the "materiality" of the body? If we speak in Lacanian terms, "materiality" is, again,
a conceptual product, an invention of language. That is why when we
attempt to refer to the absolute out there outside of language, we refer
only to the sheer experience or the empirical effects of the instance
called the real.

This implication is the necessary result of the operation of the binary
by which Butler's theory is determined. It is a direct consequence of
the repetitive reaffirmation of the opposition between fiction (fantasy)
and reality (she uses all three terms: "reality," "real," "what is true"). The
opposition implies the conflicting situatedness of the two terms vis-à-
vis each other representing two irreconcilable domains. If the relation
of opposition has such a defining, constitutive status, the conclusion
that the two domains are irreconcilable is unavoidable. Moreover, Butler clearly relates the domain of "reality" to the real in psychoanalytic
terms, that is, to sex as the reality of the body and of materiality. Nonetheless, this implication is immediately superseded by an "imaginarization" of the body or of the material that is imposed precisely by the
need to transcend their status as the unthinkable and impossible (site
of existence).

Butler's solution to the state of aporia created by the binary of the
real and fiction consists in the "philosophical decision" that would be
qualified by Laruelle as Nietzschean.[31] The act of "imaginarization in

advance" of the real implies the following: fiction = reality; reality = fiction; these equations are situated in a vicious circle.[32] As mentioned above, the great circle (of the eternal return) is indeed one of the great metaphors of Nietzsche's philosophical project of discovering the door that leads outside of the aporetic entrapment of metaphysical thought. I am subscribing here to Laruelle's comment regarding this type of solution: "the form of the equation has been changed, but the equation as a form of thought still persists."[33] According to Laruelle, this "romantic" solution is, in fact, an "escape in advance into fiction [*une 'fuite en avant' dans la fiction*]."[34] What is even more important and fundamentally problematic concerning this type of solution is that the binary structure of opposites persists, and the play between its two components remains within the unshakeable constraint of oppositional duality (dualism).

Through our reading of the passage from Judith Butler's *Bodies That Matter*, seen as a procedure of exposure of the aporetic situation between construction and reality one finds in constructivism, I am proposing a deconstruction of the couple of reality and fiction (as a couple) and of its nature of opposition. This is an invitation to abandon the dualistic picture of the real and its shadow, or, in different words, to claim the reality of what in the quoted paragraph by Butler is called "fiction." This claim is enunciated through a posture of thought modeled according to Laruelle's method of a Vision-in-One, where fiction and the real are not opposed. They are not even placed into a relation that would condition their respective meanings.

Liberated from the constraints of a philosophical decision—according to which we are inevitably urged to think fiction as contrary to reality or in a binary mutual hold with it—the reality that is unconditioned by fiction or the processes of the Imaginary, of signification, or of thought becomes possible. The reality of the mental, intellectual, psychic, and bodily productions, the reality of the constructions or creations of human and nonhuman, becomes real in its singularity, as nonopposed and radically unrelated to any other (more) accomplished reality. Reality that is not conditioned by fiction "performs" as the real; it affirms its internal laws of constitution, which are not negotiable within the "microcosmos"; it creates, and within the "cosmos" (or the Laruellian world) it participates in.

By nonnegotiable I mean impossible to be subjected to dismissal through discursive intervention, for example, a radical critique that would declare them redundant or irrelevant, without resulting into the demise of the entire world (of the self). The only thing that is ultimately nonsubjectable to deconstruction is that which in its last instance escapes language: the nonreflected experiential, the excess of *the lived* (Laruelle's *vécu*) through the utter singularity of one's being in the world. I am therefore referring to the ultimate limitations of arbitrariness of thought, which are dictated by the lived. The lived escapes articulation through language, and yet again it is ultimately relevant for liveability itself—and therefore for the "legitimacy" or "legislative power"—of all linguistic constructions that our world is made of.

Therefore, the reality of the "fictional constructions" such as sex and gender, which have the role of determining our lives—or even making them possible—as their necessities, works as Dilthey's real. That is to say, by virtue of being life-constituting necessities, these fictions, in the last instance, will enact resistance to the individual will or to the intentionality of the subject. The subject is always already and inescapably *assujeti*, *subjected* (from the Latin *sub-iectus*, derived from the verb *ub-icio*, "to fall under") to these fictions. It is *subjected* to the rule of these necessities inasmuch as it is "life enabling." (Butler says that "without them life would be unthinkable.") And, then again, the subject and its survival are possible precisely as the result of the liveability delivered by these very limitations to its "free will."

The discursive constructs that life is based on and carried out through contain an aspect that renders them a necessity, an instance that is ultimately compulsory and not negotiable—a limit, a limit to arbitrariness. Thus, there are aspects of discursiveness that produce the effect of the real in its role as the impenetrable frontier (limit) of language. Also, according to Heidegger, the "experience of resistance," "the unveiling of the Resistant," is what characterizes the "in-the-World-Existent" (or "Being"), or, to use the original term, *Innerweltliche eiende*.[35] And this very experience of resistance (from the "outside world") ensues and becomes an experience and consciousness of reality, which is itself, in a way, a mode of Being-in-the-World (*in-der-Welt-sein*), says Heidegger.[36]

Butler's "fictional constructions," in their role of *life-conditioning* and *nonnegotiable* necessities, echo the psychoanalytic real as the nonpenetrable (by meaning), as the impact of *tuché*[37] on the *automaton* (the signifying chain). In this sense, they also conform with the Laruellian real, in its sense of "finitude radicale,"[38] and also with the Laruellian other (*l'Autre*) liberated from the authority of the same (*le Même*)—the real in its reality of singularity and absoluteness.[39]

THE REAL REAFFIRMED (UNILATERALLY)

Resistance Revisited

The fact that the constructions made of fantasy act in a certain—or rather, the last—instance as an impenetrable, insurmountable, non-negotiable limit that is the real itself implies another fact, that the subject's capacity for and "authority" over its auto-reinventions is intrinsically limited. The subject is subjected to the rule of the "constructed world" which—in the last instance—installs itself as an acting real vis-à-vis the intentionality of the self to reinvent it (and itself). The self is ultimately limited in its workings of autotransformation also by the rule of the real, which is most directly enacted by the pure labor of self-preservation of the (human) individual as the continuity of the self-identical "I" (as I have attempted to demonstrate in the previous chapter of this book).

I shall reiterate my argument elaborated in the previous chapter: it is possible to conceive of a unity for a nonunitary subject without reintroducing the classical idea and ideal of the autonomous subject. On the contrary, insisting on the presence and the relevance of the instance of oneness—which implies continuity and a specific mode of unity for the self—reaffirms self's ultimate vulnerability and constitutive dependence on the "world."

Finally, it is significant to note that the limit, that is, the real, which "lives" both in that which is exterior to the subject and in its utmost interiority, is characterized as resistance by almost all of the authors mentioned in this chapter: Butler, Heidegger, Dilthey, and Laruelle. The limit is, therefore, the site of resistance. It is the conditioning necessity of our lives and also the topos of resistance. It is the foundation of normality and of its critique. Depending on whether it is situated in the exteriority or in the interiority of the self, it is either the resistance of the "outside world" to the individual subject's intervention or vice versa, the subject's resistance to the intervention of the "world."

"P.S.": The Anxiety of the Unreal

About a decade after the publication of *Bodies That Matter*, Judith Butler, in *Undoing Gender* from 2004, argued for affirmation of the status "real" for an individual or a group. In it, "to be real" becomes a question of political recognition. To be "derealized," to be unreal, is the result of political annihilation. Rendering an individual or a group unreal is a means of brutal political repression. The discursive erasure of the name and the speech of an individual or collective self produces its complete silencing; its removal from the political agora is an act of exclusion from the political field. And when their voices finally reach us they are noise to us, since their speech and what they are "makes no sense" to us; it's outside the realm of the humanely conceivable (according to our image of humanity). They remain unnoticed, unrecognized, and incomprehensible—they are unreal to us.

Political emancipation or winning political rights and power consists in the conquering of the domain of realness by those who are rendered unreal, that is to say, those who are denied the most fundamental recognition by society not only in terms of their rights but also in terms of their existence as participation in the reality. Butler has relentlessly argued in all of her writings for recognition of the marginalized and repudiated by the normalizing society. The recognition she has always advocated does not only concern the (human) *rights* of the invisible.

It has also always already been a claim for the affirmation of the identitary difference as one that calls upon rethinking and transforming the norms. In *Undoing Gender*, she resorts for the first time to the concept of the "real" and of the "unreal" as central terms of political and ethical relevance in her argumentation. Together with the notion of the real, the concepts of the "limit" and "survival" are elemental for the rhetoric of this book. This is a shift in naming that deserves our attention here. Naming is situating in language. Consequently, the shift implies that the problems have received a different status and different content in her work after 2000. *Precarious Life* from 2006 and *Frames of War* from 2009 confirm and reinforce the shift in Butler's language toward granting greater relevance to the status and sense of "being real" (regardless of whether this sense is discursively produced) in her political or politico-ontological discourse.

This change is reflected in her insisting on the importance not only of the discursive but also of the nonreflected or prelinguistic experienced—that is, in the sense of being perceived (by the others and in the "world")—as real. The sense or even sensation of one's own and other's "realness" for and in the "world" is now a key element in the operation of political recognition and also for attaining and preserving the status of a recognized subjectivity (and not only an identity).

So it is not just that a discourse exists in which there is no frame and no story and no name for such a life, or that violence might be said to realize or apply this discourse. Violence against those who are already not quite lives, who are living in a state of suspension between life and death, leaves a mark that is no mark. If there is a discourse, it is a silent and melancholic writing in which there have been no lives, and no losses, there has been no common physical condition, no vulnerability that serves as the basis for an apprehension of our commonality, and there has been no sundering of that commonality. None of this takes place on the order of the *event*. None of this takes place.[40]

And such lives (for example, "those who live outside the conjugal frame or maintain modes of social organization for sexuality that are neither monogamous nor quasi-marital"), which are no lives leaving a "mark that is no mark" (in the discursive and also as an "event" in the Badiousian sense), are, according to Butler, "considered unreal."[41] *Undoing Real* is a book that relies heavily on the underlying conviction that to be considered unreal is the most brutal form of oppression; it is presented not only as annihilation of the very fundament for claiming any (human) rights (namely, in order to claim rights one has to "be there," to exist, to participate in the "reality"), but also as the most debasing, cruel act of an attempted effacement "in the real" of the real of one's existence: it is the ultimate and inexorable form of oppression in itself. In this way, one performs a gesture of annihilation of the real as *lived* (in the Laruellian sense). It attempts to erase the materiality or the bodily aspects of the experience of the "unreal people": the enjoyed and the suffered (in Laruelle, both of them are encompassed by the term "le joui").[42] As Butler says, "their loves and losses [are considered] less than 'true' loves and 'true' losses. The derealization of this domain of human intimacy and sociality works by denying reality and truth to the relations at issue."[43] The claim for social recognition and change is at the same time a claim to realness, an endeavor to attain—or perhaps conquer—the domain of reality. In this sense, Realness is not an Imaginary category that can appear as a mere "device" of the Symbolic, whose aim is to enable social recognition. The right to realness becomes a right in itself.

Conquering the domain of "knowable reality" means something more than "a simple assimilation by the prevailing norms"; it is a change that entails discrete and unpredictable transformations in the ruling normativity itself (precisely as the effect of the intervention of the unruly real into the intelligible reality). Butler writes: "To intervene in the name of transformation means precisely to disrupt what has become settled knowledge and knowable reality, and to use, as it were, one's unreality to make an otherwise impossible or illegible claim. I think that when the unreal lays claim to reality, or enters into its domain, something other than a simple assimilation into prevailing norms can and does take place."[44] It seems that in *Undoing Gender* there appears a difference of critical significance, the one between recognition through discourse or as "discursive reality" and the one that she calls "entering the domain of reality" as a politico-ontological instance. Butler's habitual claim, especially in the 1990s, was that reality is always already made possible precisely through discourse. Nonetheless, this claim has evidently been appended or expanded and reinforced in *Undoing Gender* by the insisting on the status of realness as ultimately legitimating (one's identity and rights). And realness is that which belongs to the domain of the "liveable" and to "embodiment." "Liveability" is an instance on which Butler strongly insists in this book, and it is inherently related to the statuses of "realness" and "humaneness": "it is one thing to assert the reality of lesbian and gay lives as a reality, and to insist that these lives are worthy of protection in their specificity and commonality; but it is quite another to insist that the very public assertion of gayness calls into question what counts as reality and what counts as a human life."[45] Hence, "to be called unreal . . . is one way in which one can be oppressed."[46] Realness is, therefore, a question of liveability, or a question related in an intrinsic way to "the tasks of persistence and survival."[47] In this text, we can notice Butler constantly connecting the questions of survival,[48] of realness, and of the "I" (instead of the "subject") to those of political and social recognition. This line of reasoning reintroduces the question of opposition between reality and fantasy, and this time the opposition is resolved through a theoretical move consisting in an affirmation of the interrelatedness of the two notions as fundamentally nonoppositional:

> Fantasy is not the opposite of reality; it is what reality forecloses, and, as a result, it defines the limits of reality, constituting it as its constitutive outside. The critical promise of fantasy, when and where it exists, is to challenge the contingent limits of what will and will not be called reality. Fantasy is what allows us to imagine ourselves and others otherwise; it establishes the possible in excess of the real; it points elsewhere, and when it is embodied, it brings elsewhere home.[49]

Here, one can notice a significant shift in the way of thinking each of the two notions and the ways in which they relate with each other. They are clearly no longer paralyzed by an oppositional and mutually conditioning interrelatedness. Fantasy defines "the limits of reality," "constituting it as its constitutive outside," but in a sense that calls into play the reality in order to become the "possible in excess of the real." This is a discourse on how the two instances relate, but one that allows a possibility of thinking each of the notions in their singularity. Fantasy has a "life of its own"; it is an ultimately autonomous instance generating life that will one day conquer the territory of what is considered real. Their relation is no longer mutually exclusive: when the fantasized "elsewhere" is *embodied*, it brings elsewhere home.

Fantasy is brought back home, into the real. Fantasy is translatable into the real, and yet it can live an independent life since, in the last instance, it is not defined by translatability. In *Undoing Gender*, the relation between the two notions is considered, but the consideration itself is not relationist. There does not seem to be any aporetic self-entrapment of thought since there is no underlying circularity at work.

I am referring to a circularity of the kind where the translation of the one term into the other means its disappearance into it, an engulfment of the first by the second. I am referring to those ceaseless workings of the speculative mind (in Irigaray's sense) that necessarily bring in an establishing of a cycle of mutual effacement of the two concepts.

The mutual effacement is carried out either by the exclusion of the other term or by its total inclusion, which comes down to an utter appropriation (by the other term), to a "colonization" of the one term by the other. In *Undoing Gender*, however, Butler's thinking seems to be relieved of this unnecessary burden. Her discourse here is discharged from that hard labor of thought that does not bring to life anything but an endless intermirroring of two notions. Here, her thought is free from the tiresome cyclicality of the narcissistic thought instituting sameness through otherness and invasions of each other.

3

ON THE LIMIT AND THE LIMITLESS

THE BAN OF THE LIMIT

Our postmodern era defines itself as such on the basis of its pretension to having transcended the relevance of some old metaphysical notions, which have been habitually reduced to the Cartesian philosophical legacy and its language. These are not only concepts that ought to be seen as having been proven redundant for the postmodern considerations of the world (in the Laruellian sense) or the universe(s) of humanity. It also seems that, apart from acquiring the status of methodological and ontological redundancy, they have also become anathema on "moral grounds." Namely, they have become "bad words": the one and the real have come to be equated with fixedness, stability, and continuity (nontransformability). These notions, on the other hand, have been identified and reduced to the core of conservative political values: one implies unification and unification implies imperialist universalism, realism implies the violence of positivism, and fixedness and stability intimate the heteronormative and patriarchal essentializing of the historically conditioned gender positions. It is true that throughout the history of the Western speculative mind, these words have acquired oppressive political value. However, it is also true that these words can assume different positions in language and that it is therefore ridiculous to throw them out as something anathema. The anathema consists in the fact that they have been practically banned from what presents itself nowadays as the contemporary theory of "humanity," that is, transcendental universes that simultaneously constitute and explain the world.

These are all words that have been "derealized" (in Butler's sense, as explained in the previous chapter), relegated to the realm of the unthinkable and the impossible for any thought that pretends to be one of authority in these postmodern times. For non-standard philosophy (which is yet another name for non-philosophy), words also establish a positive reality, one that can be rigorously studied. Therefore, the thought that has declared these words "outlandish" (unthinkable or irrelevant) has also determined them as that which is outside the language and the accessible, that is, possible reality. These are names, concepts that are banned from the discourse that purports to have done away—or to have to a large extent progressed along that way—with the metaphysical constraints of thought.

The ontological and political all-inclusiveness of poststructuralist discourses is based on the exclusion of these several names. I am referring to the postmodern fascination with the construction of open fields of free play of thought (discourse, text), of transience of meanings and situations, of the rhizome-like bundle of traces behind the deconstructed arbitrariness (a notion, a discourse, a social, cultural, or psychological structure, and so on). Surely this is a generalization and clearly a reductionist view, since, for example, behind Derrida's "playful textuality" there also exists the very rigorous structure of his ethical thought, the backbone of his philosophy.[1] Also, behind the "rhizomaticity" of Deleuze's thought in *L'Anti-Oedipe* (*Anti-Oedipus*) and *Mille Plateaux* (*A Thousand Plateaus*) there lies a meticulously constructed ontology of unilateral difference and pure affirmation, which is elaborated in *Différence et répétition* (*Difference and Repetition*).

The ambivalent position of Derrida regarding such fundamentally metaphysical concerns and their constitutive role in any pertinent ontology is illustrated through the correlation between the following two quotations taken from Jane Flax's *Thinking Fragments* (1991): "Derrida's deconstruction of the misrepresentation of the Real presupposes and depends upon his own, often covert ontological premises. For him the Real does have a (mystical) essence. It is heterogeneous, infinitely open, and governed by chance. The philosopher's task is to invoke rather than present the Real."[2] This is a comment on Derrida's invocation of the real in his discourse—as something in a seeming contradiction with the main enterprises of postmodernism—which Flax gives immediately after having proposed her general claim about postmodern thought (in general): "Postmodernism is a valuable form of discipline philosophers impose on themselves. Postmodernists generate intra-discourse warnings and limitations: No, you can't do that. That way lies grandiosity, illusion, the seductive tyranny of metaphysics, truth, the real."[3]

I agree with Flax's assertion about postmodernism generating "intra-discourse warnings and limitations" that are directed precisely against the "real," among other notions (as I myself have argued at more length in the first chapter of this book). Certainly, it is not every kind of an "intra-discourse warning" that is equally attributable to each and every textual corpus that comes under the rubrics of "postmodernism" and "poststructuralism," as we can see from the example above, which shows that one of the emblematic figures of postmodernism believes in (or "invokes") the discursive pertinence of the real. The qualifications produced by Flax concerning "postmodernism"—qualifications I subscribe to—refer more often to something that one might call the postmodernist intellectual habitus (and the textual legacy it creates, in particular through its reception in the United States). They are not always applicable to the ensemble of the most significant texts that are normally put under the label of postmodernism.

Still, I will argue that in spite of some critical differences—reflecting both the fact that there is no monolithic poststructuralism and the belief that behind the purporting of all-reigning arbitrariness there still persists an ambition to determine some *Arché*-of-All-Being—playful vicissitudes are something that has been inaugurated into *the* ideology of the postmodern era. The acceptance of this ideology bestows correctness in thought and acting, which are accommodated to the ruling ontologies of our time(s): pseudomaterialist, pragmatist, poststructuralist, and neoliberal truths about the nonexistence of stable truths and meanings that imply uncertainty as the fundament of all existence.

The declaration of the "death of certainty" is a position common to all poststructuralist texts of authority (and recognized as relevant to and representative of the centers of intellectual and academic power), regardless of the above-mentioned significant differences. The installation of this "truth" has produced an entire habitus, not only an intellectual and academic one, but also one of lifestyle(s). Or, to quote Jane Flax (who embraces much of the philosophy and methodology of what is usually called postmodernism and poststructuralism while still preserving the position of an un-self-censored critic of the intellectual trend it creates): "postmodernists construct their own meta-narratives of the 'death' of the Enlightenment or the 'metaphysics of presence,' thus violating their own principles of 'defferal' and indeterminacy. Reason (this time disguised as 'language') reappears, persistently pursuing its cunning plan, despite the apparent dominance of entropic forces in the world."[4]

In a sense, by way of inaugurating vicissitudes and uncertainty as the sole possible certainty, crisis is affirmed and legitimated as the only stability. But at the same time, by way of inaugurating it as the sole reality, uncertainty has been domesticated, stabilized, and perverted into its paradoxical (acting) opposite. For some of us, "the children of postmodern culture and academism," in spite of its benefaction, this position—as the only "acceptable," the only "right position"—has also been able to produce a rather uncomfortable existential settling. Discomfort is mainly generated by the fact that the "discovery" of the essential uncertainty has in effect been—or has practically acted as—a positively determined ontological truth about the "essence of being." The impermeability of this truth causes the naïve or infantile yet spontaneous reaction to the Imaginary, creating a phantasm about the world of vertiginous instability as the only possible world.[5] The emotional transposition of this sort of ideological setting is anxiety.[6] It issues from the totality of a single possibility—that of the absolute, irreversible truth about the irrevocable and essential uncertainty.

The advantageous side of this unique ontological possibility is its aspect of continuous change, its ceaseless mobility—the open horizon of overwhelming, omnipresent possibility. Here one can notice the overlapping of the poststructuralist and postmodern optimisms with those of neoliberalism regarding the inexhaustible, never-ending existence of possibilities. Futurist fundamentalism is a trait they have in common.

Judith Butler is right when she says that placing so many different theoretical trends and authors of utterly different and often opposing visions—the heterogeneous ensemble of names such as Lacan, Foucault, Derrida, Kristeva, Irigaray, Cixous, and others—under the same rubric of poststructuralism and postmodernism is an inaccurate generalization.[7] Nonetheless, I argue, the theoretical productions associated with the label of poststructuralism and postmodernism, that is, the academic commentarisms created around its "founding figures," do have something in common. Notably, it is the belief in the ceaseless possibility of a purely linguistic universe or the reality of completely objectified materiality devoid of relevance (unless "signified"). It is a reality based on the exclusion of the real, the negative, the absence, and death from the immortal play of discursiveness. Immortality (consisting in the "ceaselessness of possibility") accorded to the—always already discursive—reality results in a particular and peculiar pathology of that same reality.

Namely, the oversaturation of possibility is equal to an entropy of positivity of our times, as Baudrillard diagnosed, resulting in a suffocating omnipresence of simulacra as the only reality of our postmodern times. It is the only reality recognized as reality, a subterfuge of the real, acting in its stead. It conditions what happens in the lingual universe by mimicking the effect of the Real (in the Lacanian sense). In *Symbolic Exchange and Death*,[8] Baudrillard invokes the affirmation of negativity or death as the cure to the entropy of reality. To avoid the paths of argumentation that might make Baudrillard's claim, and my subscription to it, resonate as mystical ontology, let me just say that the overwhelming evidence about the ruling interdiction of the negative (hence, death and its traces) that *Symbolic Exchange and Death* gives is telling. One recognizes the suppression, the denial, the evident censorship of the "no," death, and loss—the annihilation of the limit. The only permitted reality is that of the endless expansion of the positive. Through the denial of the limit, one has attempted to deny or cancel the reality of finitude, of that which introduces absence (of possibility or naming) and the concomitant experience of utter and radical frustration of thought.

Considering the materialist background of the thought based on the ban of the negative, finitude, and the a priori impossibility of enveloping the real by thought—and of transcending the limit it poses or the limit it is—are recognized and granted legitimacy. Nonetheless, and paradoxically, precisely as a result of this recognition, they are instantaneously expelled from discursiveness all together. This is paradoxical because it seems that this radical deficiency of thought automatically translates itself into a certain positively determined constitutive "essence" which is total(izing). It seems that the recognition of the nonabsoluteness of thought translates itself into an absolute verdict according to which thought itself is fundamentally constituted by this particular impossibility.

In other words, the statement "thought can only mediate a certain 'real' but never encompass and grasp it in its entirety" automatically, or by means of a certain intrinsic rule of the system of thought, translates itself into the following absolutist statement: "thought in itself is always already incapable to communicate the real." Thus, "a certain real," which can also be read as "any real" (and which implies its multiplicity), is transformed into the unique, monolithic, absolute, and immutable real. Plurality and mobility of thought has been suspended precisely through the fixing of thought to *the* thought defined by the relation of opposition it establishes with the real, in spite of the fact that postmodern theory defines thought as utter linguistic arbitrariness. Therefore, the postmodern and poststructuralist free flow of discursiveness is produced through this process of thinking's coagulation into the aporetic construct of "thought as absolute arbitrariness." Through this inconspicuous reversal of thought, the absolute recognition of the limit and the real has been turned into its contradicting counterposition of utter suspension of the limit and the real. At the same time, the impotency of thinking has been transformed into thought's omnipotence. The real is banned from the clean territory of the immaterial, autoreproducing thought.

Let us concentrate on the suspension of the limit as one of the first names of the real or as one of the determinations in the last instance of the real. Let us consider the interdiction of the very possibility of a frontier, or rather the ban of an affirmed boundary (instead of its ceaseless and "immanently" unstoppable postmodern crossing). In this way, we will be able to evade the danger of "frontal confrontation" with the multilayered difficulty of deconstructively approaching the fortified inviolability of the notion of the real as the unthinkable. Unthinkable is a qualification that the poststructuralist rendering of Lacan has stipulated as its axiomatic presupposition. My reading of Lacan's theory of the real is different. And it is close to Žižek's understanding of the position of the real in Lacan's theory[9] and to that of Alenka Zupančič.[10] I believe that Lacan's real has a significantly more complex and active position with respect to language than the reductionist poststructuralist readings believe it does.

The limit as the "no" to endless signification, the limit as the unbridgeable lack lingering in every difference, the real of absence between two realities is *always already* superseded by an act of transcendence. Such an act would consist of the compulsory and simultaneous gesture of interpretation in terms of an affirming difference (a gesture conditioned by the internal structural regulations of the language itself). In the framework of the dominant ideologies of the postmodern era, affirmation of difference is always already its transcendence, and never affirmation of the abyss upon which any difference resides.

There seems to be a consensus in poststructuralist discourses, including poststructuralist feminism, that the reality of this gap, the frustration created by the hindering abyss (of the negative) cannot be subject to thought, cannot be encompassed by or introduced into discursiveness. Its ontological status places it in the realm of the *au-delà*, of the certain "beyond" that is an ontological actuality per se. The gap of absence (of language) is declared nonexistent or, to put it in terms closer to Laruelle's non-standard philosophy, "not-there." One cannot translate it into language. Therefore, it is not. This is the so-called postmodern position (and condition).

It is the utter limitation, the irrevocable and absolute "no" that is discursively untranslatable and relegated to the realm of the impossible, not the one that is interpreted as the affirmed "différance" which can be affirmed (that is, the "always already crossed" border, margin, and so forth). In poststructuralist and poststructuralist feminist theory, it is the name of the real that holds this position, not the name of the limit. Nevertheless, the latter is the aspect of the poststructuralist, banished real that I am interested in, since I would like to call upon a legitimization of the reality of the ultimate "No" (of a certain real or of the real). Or, in Laruelle's terminology, it is the limit as one of "the first names of the real"[11] that I would like to investigate as well as its status in poststructuralist (feminist) theory. Arguing for this, I will invoke discursive "legitimacy" and relevance for the instance of the limit in and for feminist theory. I will invoke a discourse that incorporates the realities of limitation without having them *always already* transposed into the "transcendental real" (the fixed abstraction out there), recognizing them as inherent constituents of its overall experience and conceptualization of reality. I would like to reclaim the neglected truth that the unstoppable flux of autoproliferating textuality has always already found itself in and founded itself upon the relentless, never-ceding grasp of creative opposition with the (disclaimed) real, or rather, with its ultimate limit(s).

This continuous, founding defiance of discourse vis-à-vis the ultimate or absolute limitations (that is, those that are utterly unchangeable, unbendable, impossible subjects to negotiations), vis-à-vis the limit determined in the last instance as castration, has been the provocation for the postmodern inflation of signification. Nonetheless, creativeness and productivity, these great values of both postmodernism and neoliberalism, created out of the frustration imposed by the real, have never been fully realized as a ceaseless "free flow" of discursiveness and textuality. In different words, all of these *effects* of the real upon language are *events* occurring in the world of discursiveness that remain without names. The only names they have been given are the ones fixing them as unnameable. These events are instances and operations within discourse that do not enter the register of naming. And beyond the text they remain. The ban of the real from discursiveness debilitates or prohibits any discussion of its immediate or mediated effects: limitation, trauma, unmediated crisis, frustration, negation, and death, which are *operative* within language and discourse.

Let us engage with another neglected aspect of the instance of the real—its multiplicity and its suppression by poststructuralism. There is but one real—the Lacanian Real. It is ungraspable and transcendental. The poststructuralist real is the absolute real. Namely, if (in the poststructuralist context) the real is a name for an ontological status not substantiated as some (mystical) entity, then why is the possibility of the multiplicity of its manifestations excluded as the subject of thematization? Surely, one can speak of discursive *events*—to put it in a rather free appropriation of Badiou's parlance—since the event of the (auto)imposition of a certain episteme as the foundation for a certain discursive cosmos is an act, a gesture. Or, resorting to Schmitt's terminology as laid out in *Political Theology*,[12] the introduction of a new law (theoretical or scientific) is an act of violence and an enactment of sovereignty of the "legislating" authority of a doctrine. The gesture itself, the event of imposition or of the act of installation of a certain axiom as grounding for the discursive "world" that is grounded in it, demonstrates the effect of the real. Its effectuation is an instance of the real. It is a thrust into the reality as we have known it until that moment, a traumatic intervention that will transform the image of the world. The multiplicity of events that constitute the instance of the real is an aspect (of the real) that is also suppressed, invisible, unrecognized in postmodern theorizing. Such an utterance would sound absurd, since the real is always referred to in the singular. The multiple eventality of the real is never approached as such, but has always already been obliterated through its reduction to the generalizing notion of some "Ur-" real.

Let us resort to Alain Badiou's concept of the "evental site" in order to explain the multiple substantiation of the real and, hence, its onto-mathematical status of multiplicity. The status does not exclude the singular aspect or status of the real. Both aspects are considered unilaterally. The evental site is a position held by social groups or categories of subjectivity that are virtually nonexistent for the "situation" (a concept analogous to Laruelle's world) whose inhabitants they are. They are on the edge of the void (the real) upon which the situation resides. And for the language that the situation disposes with, they remain unrepresentable. In fact, these groups hold the position of the void, *they are* the void for the situation they inhabit, but when they act and thereby create an entirely new truth, they do it from the position of the evental site. The evental site is still part of "the situation," albeit on its edge and bordering with the void. Badiou speaks of the proletariat as inhabitants of the void in the time of Marx, and of the "hysterical feminists" and the Middle East "terrorists" as inhabitants of the void in our time (situation).[13] Therefore, the real—or the void—in terms of Badiou's philosophy of the event has many faces, many "representatives." In conclusion, it is *multiple*. Its instantiations as events are experienced as singularity.

To illustrate the point, let us consider the following example, which is symptomatic of the suppression I am problematizing here and present in contemporary social theory. The entire quest for a fair society, with "equality" and "freedom" as the main principles of societal organization, led by the proponents of what is *recognized*[14] as the legitimate political thought of today, is founded upon a consensus based on an arbitrariness that holds the status of an absolute, namely, the one according to which the normative society must be "democratic." (It is arbitrariness in the sense of its historic contingency and the philosophical decision of the dominant political subjectivity.) Furthermore, it seems that according to some internal laws of the existing political discourses of recognized legitimacy, the choice of this particular arbitrariness (over some possible others) to appear as normative on an international scale has never been tackled by the deconstructivists. (This attitude is in tune with the postmodern strategy and ideological determination of avoiding the metaphysical traps of the "big questions" that might open some of the infamous "grand narratives.")

It remains a fact that we are dealing with a discursive construct that evades any deconstruction. Surely, the concepts of "the democratic" and "democracy" are amply thematized and problematized. Still, its undisputed position of axiomatic necessity for any social and political organization that participates in the reality called "contemporary political order" and its status of a horizon, its aspect of conditioning necessity, is beyond discourse. One is aware that there are also nondemocratic societies, but they are defined only relationally with respect to democracy. It is the limit of discursivity, and all available political discourses of today revolve around it. It *acts* as the real for the discourses in question and for their subjects.

The conditioning powers of the chief presupposition of a discourse are, as a rule, unquestioned; the origins of the discourse of a more or less defined physiognomy are not discussed. They are not recognized as the real representing the ultimate limitation to discursiveness. Yet this limit is made of discursiveness: that which plays the role (or assumes the status) of the real in linguistic constructs. This situation speaks both of the particularistic, thus multiple, "nature" of the real—which has been neglected or negated as such by the discourses of postmodernism—and of the overlooked creative powers of one of its defining aspects, namely, the limit. Limit is one of the first names of the real, in the Laru-ellian sense and in spite of the fact that it does not appear on any of Laruelle's "lists" of possible first names. Namely, there is no such list as a list, or, let's say, "the list" is never closed and the first name of the real is a concept affected by the immanence of an aspect of the real or an instantiation of it. In *Théorie générale des victims*,[15] Laruelle explains that the very fact that the idea of humanity has been taken to its limit and that in that process the human has been disintegrated facing its disappearance, "humanism," or the necessity to determine the human-in-human reemerges.[16]

It reveals the fact about a constitutive fissure in any discursiveness, in the discursiveness itself, and the fact that a new discourse arises only from a fundamental crisis inside of it, a crisis of language that borders muteness (and sometimes transgresses that border). Therefore, it is not only the great silence over the great, ineffable real that we detect here; we also detect the silence about the origin and the discursively generat-ing powers of a particular original presupposition and its relegation to the realm of the real that one does not speak of.

Let us consider these cracks of constitutive lack within discourse, the scarred face of discourse, scarred by negativity, by impossibility, by the "unthinkable" which has been relegated to the realms outside language. Even if this banishment is not produced by the language of the old metaphysics, it ought to be considered metaphysical because it operates as an absolute exclusion of and transposition to the level of the abstract, which is unattainable in its ontologically independent transcendental life. Thus, one of the constitutive discursive moves of poststructuralist (feminist) thinking is the unreserved affirmation of the presence of the real (which absurdly manifests itself, but as absence) and its engulfing potency, together with the affirmation of the utter impotence of thought with regard to it. The real is affirmed only in order to announce its derealization and initiate the endless festival of discursive omnipotence. Conspicuously, the compulsive insisting on the real's untameable potency serves only as an apotropaic strategy (naming that serves to avert its "evil powers") in order to introduce the merry vision of a world in which everything is discourse. It is a vision of a world in which the real under its first name of the limit lives no more. It "intervenes" through the "cracks" in signification. Nonetheless it intervenes as the "uncanny" external.

LACANIAN EXCURSION

We find ourselves in an ontopolitical setting that can be defined as a neurotic ceaseless demand for a "guarantee of truth" almost a century after it was described by Lacan in his paper "Au-délà du 'Principe de réalitié,'" published in 1936. The search for a "guarantee of truth" that marks "contemporary psychology and philosophy" can only be transcendental, "even when the philosopher has just denied its existence," claims Lacan (referring to the denial of the existence of the transcendental).[17] Paradoxically, it is precisely within the framework of the Lacanian psychoanalytical legacy, that is, through the postmodernist philosophico-theoretical reception of Lacan's theory, that we have come to the point where the purported "emancipation" from the need for certitude has turned into its opposite. As I already argued, this situation is the result of the repetitive operation of rigid mutual exclusion taking place between the language and the Real.

But is this something that is part of the repertoire of Lacan's original claims? True, Lacan categorizes the Real as the impossible, as the unthinkable, but this does not mean that it does not exist *for* the language, that the real does not interact productively with the signifying chain and is, hence, an active force in the processes of discursive configurations. The insisting on this mutuality of rapport is present already in Lacan's works, such as the above-mentioned "Au-délà du 'Principe de réalité'"[18] and notably in a chapter of *The Four Fundamental Concepts of Psychoanalysis* entitled "Tuché and Automaton."[19]

First, the *tuché*, which we have borrowed, as I told you last time, from Aristotle, who uses it in his search for cause. We have translated it as *the encounter with the real*. The real is beyond the *automaton*, the return, the coming-back, the insistence of the signs, by which we see ourselves governed by the pleasure principle. The real is that which always lies behind the automaton, and it is quite obvious, throughout Freud's research, that it is this that is the object of his concern.[20]

So, it is the figure (instance) of the real lying behind the automaton that Lacan sees as Freud's chief object of interest "throughout . . . [his] research." "Freud's true preoccupation," according to Lacan, is "the question—what is the first encounter, the real, that lies behind the phantasy?"[21] Considering the position ascribed to the real vis-à-vis the signifying chain, one can infer that the question of the real has been of central relevance for psychoanalytic theory, especially that of Lacan, who "rediscovered" the question of the real and its relation to the "automaton" as Freud's "true preoccupation." Nevertheless, Lacan's self-declared devotedness to "the true Freud," his unique "heretical orthodoxy," is what gives this question the status of critical relevance for psychoanalysis tout court, and not for his own contribution to it exclusively.

Furthermore, in "Tuché and Automaton," Lacan lays out a theory about the mutual hold between "tuché" and "automaton." In other words, he creates a discourse about the real's insertion into discursiveness. It is worthwhile producing the following, perhaps lengthy quotation, which is sufficient to corroborate this claim:

> The relation to the real that is to be found in the transference was expressed by Freud when he declared that nothing can be apprehended *in effigie, in absentia*—and yet is not the transference given to us as effigy and as relation to absence? We can succeed in unravelling this ambiguity of the reality involved in the transference only on the basis of the function of the real in repetition. What is repeated, in

fact, is always something that occurs—the expression tells us quite a lot about its relation to the *tuché—as if by chance.* . . . Is it not remarkable that, at the origin of the analytic experience, the real should have presented itself in the form of that which is *unassimilable* in it—in the form of the trauma, determining all that follows, and imposing on it an apparently accidental origin?[22]

Therefore, the real makes itself present in the form of its significant and signifying absence from the signifying chain or the pleasure principle. Namely, it makes itself present not only to the transcendental form of the "paradoxical absence," but also through trauma and incidence, through that ungraspable hiatus of experience (similar to Badiou's "event"). The event (of the real) intervenes into discursiveness. It can reverse the order and logic of a discourse. It can produce an entirely different situation on the level of the pleasure principle—*it is something that happens to language.* Discursiveness builds around the event attempting to domesticate it through language. Thus, it seems that, according to Lacan, if the real in itself is unthinkable, its workings in the "world of signs" are not beyond language and discursivity.

One of the most influential representatives of Lacanian theory today, Slavoj Žižek, calls for theoretical considerations of these workings of the real. He argues about the possibility of its impact on the hegemonic (in Gramscian sense of the word) discourses of today.[23] And he is not alone in this call: *The Ethics of the Real* (2000) by Alenka Zupančič represents a brilliant example of the rich discursive possibilities originating from such a theoretical stance.

> The heart of all ethics is something which is not in itself "ethical" (nor is it "non-ethical")—that is to say, it has nothing to do with the register of ethics. This "something" goes by several different names— although we will limit ourselves to two: for Lacan, it is "the Real"; for Badiou, "the event." These terms concern something which appears only in the guise of the encounter, as something that "happens to us,"

surprises us, throws us "out of joint," because it always inscribes itself in a given continuity as a rupture, a break or an interruption. According to Lacan, the Real is impossible, and the fact "it happens (to us)" does not refute its basic "impossibility": the Real happens to us (we encounter it) *as impossible*, as "the impossible thing" that turns our symbolic universe upside down and leads to the reconfiguration of this universe."[24]

LARUELLIAN RECURSION

François Laruelle not only makes the thought of the real possible, but also claims that thinking should always already take place in accordance with the real or the one. Both terms—the real and the one—in the language of non-philosophy function as synonymous. In fact "one" is one of the "first names" of the real. Let us recall that the equation "the real = the one" stems from the status of the absolute non-relatedness of the real. The real is not only an "out there" that we encounter (in Greek τυγχάνομεν, hence τυχή or *tuché*) as a limit. The human-in-human, radical, and prelingual humanity is an experience that precedes any decision, any postulate of the thetic thought or of philosophy—it is an instance of the real. Also, the real under its first names of the lived (*le vécu* or *le joui-sans-jouissance*) is "an immanence that takes pleasure only (from) itself and solely (from) itself without outdoing itself, embarking upon or transcending itself."[25] The real is "an identity that is nothing-but-singular," and not "singular and universal" (which is to say "mixed," that is, in relation with an imagined, philosophically produced world).

Thus, the real as "the one" can be conceptualized as that which language and thought correlate to but do not reflect. In its non-philosophical posture, thought escapes the trap of entering the play with the real of mutually constituting each other. Namely, "language can describe the one, which has not at all the same structure as it, without reflecting it exactly or reproducing it."[26] Furthermore: "One would say it is a nonthetic Reflection (of the) real, a nonspecular reflection or without mirror, or a 'description in the last instance only' of the one."[27] If we suspend the philosophical decision and, consequently, the dualistic thinking as intrinsic to any philosophy, the claim about the mutual exclusion of thought and the real becomes fallacious. Thinking in terms of opposition, in binary constructs as the minimal possible structure of thought, is what—from the perspective of a non-philosophical critique—constitutes any philosophy. Philosophy is a form of thought pertaining to the "gréco-judaïque" gesture of speculation or autoreflexivity that inevitably brings about dualism as the founding feature of all philosophy. Even when dualism is purportedly transcended, for example, in Levinas or Derrida, what has actually taken place, according to Laruelle, is that "one of the opposites in the Dyad has merely been replaced by the other-which-is-not."[28] Laruelle's reference to the "gréco-judaïque" foundation of philosophy is a reference to its radical contingency, which situates it far from any rightful claim to represent the universality of thought. This claim is the opposite of "Eurocentric": it signifies that via the alleged universality of the form of thought called philosophy, the West has usurped the very possibility of a universal thought.

Furthermore, it is precisely the founding presupposition about the mutual conceptual constitution of the two opposites (the real and language), or rather their dual conceptual condition of discursive (co) existence, that makes the exclusion of the one from the territory of the other possible and necessary. This mode of thinking is enabled by the very constitutive relatedness of each of the terms and, even more so, by the necessarily binary and oppositional way of being of each of the constituents of the twofold structure; it originates from the aporetic situation in which so-called postmetaphysical thinking has found itself striving to liberate the real from the pretension of the thought that the latter constitutes the former.

Namely, this impasse (aporia) occurs as a result of the inherent impossibility of such an attempt, since the thought is *always already* constitutively grasped by the binary hold of the twofold and mutually opposing existence of the terms. To think them independently from each other is ab initio impossible. Thus, to liberate the real from the ambitions of thought means necessarily, reciprocally, and reflectively also *the opposite*—liberation of thought from any authority of the real and, thus, from any possibility of correlating with it.

One will warn against saying that language always betrays the one, because language always, as is the case, manipulates with the couples of opposites and always is the nourishing element of unitary dualities. This sort of thinking postulates that language is a specular reflection of the one, that it even has the same structure as the one (cf. the argument of the *Tractatus*), or that it is isomorphic to the one. This is a postulate of negative ontology and theology, and moreover it is a supplementary and useless presupposition: language can describe the one without having the same structure, without reflecting it exactly or reproducing it.[29]

In this view of the inherent non-relatedness of thought and the real and in both occurrences—or events—the thought and the real have singular (that is, independent and nonthetic) modes of operation. Each event of thought takes place in some mode of correspondence with the instance of the real that is unique, noncosmogonic, and noncosmologic. In this sense, one can also say that the event of thought, thought in *its aspect of an experience*, is an instance of the real in its own right. To avoid entering into the classical aporetic state of philosophical circularity, one should note that the emphasis here is on the experience of thought as event, and not on its conceptual contents that belong to the order of the transcendental.

Unlike the postmodern idea of fragment that essentially implies the fragmentation of the whole of a certain existing philosophical universe (or cosmos), the non-philosophical concept of singularity lays the ground for a "debt-free" (in relation to any previous doctrine), truly nonsystemic instance of thought. As previously explained, the real and the one are synonyms variously naming the same instance, the same thing: the singularity of the theorized reality as well as of the stance of theorizing.

The pretension to thematizing a reality in terms of its singularity, in correlation with "its real," is not a pretension to (conceptually) grasping the real, to claiming the truth of the real "as real," to being its accomplished reflection. Acknowledging its singularity and correlating with the real is an act of theoretical recognition of the "radical immanence" of the "identity" that is postulated as the "real object" of study, says Laruelle. The "real object" of study is not the real itself but a transcendental *postulate* of it. It is important that the postulate is founded upon a radical concept that is the determination in the last instance of a researched "identity."[30]

The distinction between the real (as "the finitude of identity" or its "radical immanence") and "the real object of research" does not imply the distinction between "experience and concept, the concrete and the abstract, the experimentation and the theoretical—nor any of their 'dialectizations' or 'couplings,'" insists Laruelle in *Théorie des identités*.[31] Unavoidably, the "real object" (of non-philosophical study) as a sample of the "world" contains "theorico-technico-experimental ingredients."[32] In fact, the two objects ("the real" and "the real object" of non-philosophical thinking) contain the "the same representations, but of an entirely different status."[33] Namely, the distinction between them "is not epistemological, . . . but only of-the-last-instance, that is to say, either *transcendental or immanent*," explains Laruelle.[34] It is important that the first correlates with the second, acknowledging it as the identity in the last instance of that which has been subjected to theoretical investigation, as that to which cognition subordinates itself as its ultimate authority.[35]

THE REAL AS LIMIT AND THE THOUGHT

It seems that the purported and desired unbound arbitrariness of discursiveness is a phantasmatic situatedness that has offered much *jouissance* to authorship and to writing but has never seized being in a passionate grip with the presence and absence of the real. The real is, thus, a certain "beyond the language" category that is nonetheless inherently relevant for language and discursiveness. Moreover, it is an element of language, or rather a situation of and within discourse that imposes itself as a constitutive instance and as an effect of the real, as its *conditioning limit*. This is the implicit premise of the poststructuralist beliefs concerning the categories of language and the real. Or rather, it is an implication produced by the structure itself and the internal "mechanisms" (that is, the "economy" of significations) of the conceptualization of the two notions and their interrelatedness. In fact, I will argue, following in this respect the central argument of Drucilla Cornell's *The Philosophy of the Limit*,[36] that this is a potentiality that lives in the very discursive configurations brought about by poststructuralism and postmodernism, and more specifically in the method of deconstruction.

The concept of the "philosophy of the limit" is a product of Cornell's reinventive reading of Jacques Derrida's notion of deconstruction. More accurately, it is a work of conceptual innovation issuing from her original reading of the possibilities of thought (philosophical and ethical or ethico-philosophical) that lie in the method of deconstruction and the grand ideological project of the postmodern era, which consists in the dismantling of metaphysics. If we collapse the two notions (deconstruction and the postmodern) into a single one—that of a radical critique of thought's pretension to re-presenting the real—we could say that what is at stake in "postmodernism" is the thought's repetitive affirmation of its own inherent and constitutive limitations. Cornell's "philosophy of the limit" is the fruit of her symptomatic reading and the main heuristic device of her rereading of a wider intellectual trend, namely, a vast and ranging theoretical undertaking and not only a single discursive project—that of Derrida's deconstruction. In her own words, Cornell detects and explores the possibilities of a theoretical "configuration" created by the intersection of the works of several thinkers: Jacques Derrida, Theodor Adorno, Jacques Lacan, and

Emmanuel Levinas. According to Cornell, the exposure of thought's limitations vis-à-vis "the beyond" (to it), that is to say, vis-à-vis the real, is not a nihilistic reversal of thought toward its autoforeclosure and into an aporetic paralysis. It is precisely the opposite. The "dialogue" between the following two quotations from *The Philosophy of the Limit* will show us why:

> deconstruction, reconceived as the philosophy of the limit, does not reduce the philosophical tradition to an "unreconstructable" litter, thus undermining the possibility of determining precepts for moral action; rather it exposes the quasi-transcendental conditions that establish any system. . . . This exposure, which in Derrida proceeds through what he calls the "logic of parergonality," demonstrates how the very establishment of the system as a system implies a *beyond* to it, precisely by virtue of what it excludes. The second aspect of deconstruction more accurately described by the notion of limit is related to what Charles Peirce in his own critique of Hegelian idealism called secondness. By secondness Peirce indicates the materiality that persists *beyond* any attempt to conceptualize it. Secondness, in other words, is what resists. Very simply, reality is not interpretation all the way down.[37]

The inherent impotence of thought to encompass and re-present the real in its totality is not the end of thought. It is not the truth of its meaninglessness. "The beyond" is not the closure of all thinking. On the contrary, it is a gaping opening of potentiality. Thus the limit has the ambivalent meaning of a threshold—it is both the end and the beginning of the reality of thought and language:

> The reaching of aporia for Derrida is precisely what provides us with the golden opportunity. The difference between the two thinkers [Derrida and Levinas] has to do with their approach to the beyond, the excess, the remain(s). As we will see, Derrida does recognize the

excess to established reality but only as absence that brings us to mourning.... Derrida still questions more radically than does Levinas the ability of traditional philosophical discourse to evoke the aporia of the beyond through the saying of what cannot ever be said. The recovery of the excess, the remain(s), then, is both "impossible" and necessary; impossible, and yet necessary—for to fail to pay tribute to the remains would be another violation of *heteros*.[38]

The recovery and rediscovery of these and other capacities of the philosophical gesture of deconstruction is Cornell's own work, the fruit of her own philosophical labor. The exciting move of *The Philosophy of the Limit* toward something radically new lies in the directing and resting of the philosophical glance upon an instance beyond deconstruction, in the discovery of the "time" after a "completed deconstruction." And in this sense, Cornell's philosophical preoccupations touch those of François Laruelle (and of Alain Badiou), although each of these three authors has his and her own original theoretical project with its own specific aims and means.

The limit exposed through a deconstructive gesture is a certainty of an instance that is both speechless and nameless. The acceptance of its status as ultimately (that is, in the last instance) evasive with respect to the acts of naming does not necessarily imply that one should quit attempting to grasp it, which, on the other hand, can be done only through naming. These grasps, these incomplete insights into the workings of "the limit," will generate different and many names, among them "the real" and "the one."

Drucilla Cornell claims: "To run into an aporia, to reach the *limit* of philosophy, is not necessarily to be paralyzed. We are only paralyzed if we think that to reach the limit of philosophy is to be silenced.... The dead end of the aporia, the impasse to which it takes us, promises through its prohibition the way out it seems to deny."[39] She defends this claim as much as she defends the claim that this is a possibility for thought proffered precisely by the "philosophy of the limit" of Jacques Derrida. The potentiality for an opening of and for thought created by the "dead end of aporia," which nests in the method of deconstruction, is the grounds for Cornell's naming of Derrida's theoretical legacy "a philosophy of the limit."

It is on the brink of this limit that the dimensions of language and the real interact and that one can detect thought's desire—and its under-taking—to encompass the real. Namely, each discourse is generated by a limited number of presuppositions that can be referred only to a discur-sive construct (and, more generally, to language). Language, on the other hand, ceaselessly originates from that same limited number of presuppo-sitions. The figure of this referentiality is evidently circular, and the path of argumentation is that of circularity. This is the philosophical vicious circle, the labyrinth, those haunting figures of Deleuze and Nietzsche we discussed at length in the previous chapter. A premise can be referred to and corroborated by its own product: the network that its concepts gener-ate. In other words, any discourse is purported by itself solely or by discur-siveness more generally. No instance other than itself supports it. Never-theless, it is the discourse of the real in reference to which it emerges.

Discounting recourse to evolutionism and progressivism as a way of interpretation (= construction of a history of an idea) and resorting to Foucault's concept of an episteme, let us go back to our example about democracy as the only available ideal for today's political thinking. That democracy is the only possible and thinkable principle of social organi-zation today is an inescapable presupposition—thus, an axiom—of the political reality of our time. This status (of an axiom) is intimated by the state of affairs in which it is the only acceptable (= normal and normalizing) grounding principle of the political thinking of today that has installed itself as the only legitimate one. Thus the principle of democracy is the sole "availability" for the political discourses and realities with the right to exist—everything else is abnormality that has to be policed on a global scale.

Any radical change in political thought, any movement toward a new grounding premise, is not going to take the discursive route since it is not available. In effect, the leap of thought into something utterly new and different, in its attempt to bridge the real, will be one of relative "arbitrariness." It is "relative" because one cannot claim absolute arbitrariness when what is at stake is the pursuit of discursive adequacy conditioned by the real.

When one finds oneself in the circular movement within the only and all possible discourse(s) revolving around the same grounding presupposition, there is no exceeding of the horizon. Thus, for the purposes of establishing a new horizon of thought, the cruel interruption of discursiveness is necessary. It is necessary to cease recourse to all available discourse and introduce an absolute fissure in language and an unimaginable new grounding postulation of a discourse about to be born. The source and the rise of the new horizon's wording will be again veiled by the grasp of the real. And I see this new event as open to the weaving of new narratives that will strive to approximate its reality.

4

THE REAL TRANSCENDING ITSELF
(THROUGH LOVE)

"FIDELITY," THE "RADICAL," AND THE "FIDELITY
TO THE RADICAL"

The two perhaps most influential thinkers of today's French philosophico-theoretical scene, Alain Badiou and François Laruelle, agree in their
devotedness to the project of reclaiming the thought of the radical.
Furthermore, the goal of reintroducing the relevance of the instance of
the real for the contemporary theories of the human and humanity is
another feature they have in common. Still, there are fundamental differences between the two theoretical projects. Badiou's project is radically philosophical, whereas Laruelle's is radically non-philosophical.
Badiou subscribes to the metaphysical tradition of Platonism, whereas
Laruelle rejects in advance any philosophical decision. Nonetheless,
they do share the aspiration for radicalism in method, which is routed
in a form of realism, though the routes they take in this respect are
fundamentally different, a fact made very clearly visible in Laruelle's
Anti-Badiou from 2011.[1]

The radicalism that Badiou and Laruelle have in common refers to
the theoretical positioning of fidelity to the immanence of the act of
conceptual production and its unrepeatable singularity, as well as to its
immanently autogenerated laws. The fidelity to the "act" of conceptual
production is to be read as fidelity to the "event" of truth-production
and the laws of its autoconstitution, which are immanent to this

unique event. This type of "radicalism" stands for fidelity to the reality of the unique, solitary act of thought *cor*relating with a unique, solitary instance of the real (of the theorized reality), as opposed to fidelity to a scholastic backdrop as the ultimate instance of legitimacy. This claim is appended to the one that the name, notion, and instance of the one (as in Laruelle) or the same (as in Badiou) vis-à-vis the difference have the greater theoretical productiveness or explanatory power. One of the central concerns in this sort of theoretical positioning is the attempt at "linguistic recuperation" of the real, that is to say, of creating a form within language that can inform not only about the presence and absence of the real, but also about its workings. (Badiou speaks of the void of linguistic recognizability within the "eventual site," around which a new truth, together with a new language, emerges; Laruelle invokes the radical immanence—namely, the real—as the ultimate instance of legitimization of thought.)

In spite of the critical divergences, the two thinkers have one more important argument in common. According to each of them, the act of theoretical work is always already a universalistic gesture. It is a radically individualistic (solitary), nontotalitarian, and nonuniversal(izing) (as nongeneralizing) gesture of thought. The central concern of this sort of "particularistic universalism" is to claim that the act of theorizing is always already an act of producing a "universe," one never witnessed by any other universe before. Laruelle speaks of a "language-universe," while Badiou clearly claims, "Every universal is a singularity."[2] Laruelle's "universe" is nonthetic, and it is "a dimension which is not total, but a sheer nondecisional totality."[3] In his "Thesis No. 2" on the universal, in addition to his statement that "every universal is a singularity," Badiou says: "The universal cannot be directly articulated with any recognizable particularity, grouping, or identity."[4]

In both theoretical positions there is neither the pretension to nor the epistemic possibility of "colonizing" culturally different discursivities or the subaltern, since they are both positions that see each particular instance of thinking as radically solitary or singular, striving to produce a universe and universality (of sense). There is no need to defend the position of "the fragment(al)," since when we think in terms of unilaterality or singularity we do not imagine a whole of meaning that would have undergone a process of fragmentation. The instance of "language-universe" is a product of the Vision-in-One of the representing subject, which has accomplished the process of "dialysis." This is a term from the vocabulary of Laruelle's non-standard philosophy that refers to the dismantling of the dualism inherent in philosophical language. Through dialysis we arrive at philosophical *chôra*, at a "transcendental material" and language unorganized as a discursive cosmos. The products of such a process (of thought interacting with the real) are called "language-universes," and they are "that 'final' product which is always subject to infinite reformulation and rectification," describes Laruelle.[5] Therefore, these "universes" are contingencies as well. Differently from Laruelle, Badiou presupposes the existence and universal pertinence of the ordered transcendental plane, a universe of truth(s) transcending the level of history. This vision he declares Platonic.

The prohibition, or rather the inhibition, of postmodern thought to speak of the real or the one implies and comes down to an expulsion of these "names" from the Western philosophico-theoretical vocabulary. Names are never "just" names. They are never merely linguistic phenomena once and for all defined as concepts, finite determinations, or nominal accomplishments. Notwithstanding, they have been treated by feminist poststructuralism as a certain "nominalistic real": "the stable," "the same," and "the universal" seem to have a fixed and unchanging position in poststructuralist feminist arguments that can rightfully claim the status of an unshakeable real. Their nature of inalterability within or according to the discourses in question and the fact that other categories have been excluded on the basis of the status of "virtually nonexistent" notions speak to a tacit pretension of language and thought to re-presenting the real(ity).

Through repeating of these statements, I am attempting to reiterate and reaffirm my heretical position vis-à-vis contemporary poststructuralist feminism (which includes gender and queer theory). I subscribe to a considerable part of it, while refusing to elevate its overall vision or any idea of a consistent whole of this school of thinking to having greater authority for my work than the effects of the real. I have elaborated the idea of heresy elsewhere,[6] and it is one based on Laruelle's non-standard philosophy and in particular on his *Le Christ Futur* from 2002 (translated into English in 2010). I assume the same heretical stance vis-à-vis Laruelle's non-philosophy too. I relegate the doctrine of non-philosophy to the realm of *chôra*, to the domain of the transcendental material together with that of poststructuralist feminist theorizations. Heresy that is immanent to non-philosophy originates not only from the nonorthodox stance vis-à-vis philosophy and the practice of philosophizing, but also from the epistemic and political radicalism characteristic of Christian heretic mysticism. For example, Laruelle's human-in-human suspending philosophical decision resembles Marguerite Porete's "soul which annihilates will" to find herself in the "abyss of her humility" (the human-in-human in his or her radical vulnerability).[7]

My subscription to the non-philosophical line of thinking consists primarily and fundamentally in the mere empty posture of thought that remains in fidelity to the real while *always already* facing the fact that what it has at hand is the transcendental *chôra*. While still adhering to the poststructuralist idea that we are living in a world of discursiveness and language, the empty non-philosophical posture of thought is a purposely crated crack within the always already (con)textualized thought, an opening from within the text(ure) or the language we have been made of. I see it as my "non-philosophical duty" to persevere in this posture of thought and secure a radical openness of thought. I do not find any sense in the attempt of doing away in totality with the discourses of poststructuralism and deconstruction (or of any authority relevant for the way the world sees itself today). I do not believe that anyone can yield a convincing and consistent theoretical claim to have entirely dismissed the authority of the thought shaping the epoch in which one lives. Nonetheless, one can produce a radical situating from within the situation (in Badiou's sense of the word) and, therefore, a radically different truth. But it ought to be a singular one, which cannot and does not wish to undermine the entirety of a discursive world, to replace "the system" with a new and radically different one. The radically different situating, the birth of a new truth from "the void" or from "the limit (and the real)," one taking place from within the "situation" (as in Badiou) or the "world" (as in Laruelle), can produce a dramatic shift propagating an entirely different form of discursivity and can establish a new system of thought, but it can never do so as a result of such pretension—it is always as the effect of *tuché*. Radical situating is singular, fundamentally solitary, and, therefore, immanently indifferent to such pretensions. It is "affected by immanence," and the change it can produce is one pertaining primarily to the experienced or the lived. The discursive reconfigurations cannot be predicted, although they can be desired and proffered amid the events that will take place.

To return to the question of heresy: the authorities on whose thought I will draw in the forthcoming passages, besides Laruelle and Badiou (as the principal points of reference), are Rosi Braidotti, Luce Irigaray, and Gilles Deleuze. These (at minimum) two lines of theory will meet and intertwine, establishing a dialogue between schools of thinking. The meeting of the different lines of thinking will also enable us to explore the possibilities of novel uses of language by way of creating complementing interargumentation. The ad hoc correspondences of the "philosophical and transcendental materials," regardless of their *scholastic* provenance, will be in-forming the thought that has assumed a posture of correlativity with the real. It is the consonance of the different appropriations of language echoing the experience of the real that will be filling the empty posture of thought. Thought, on the other hand, will be in an always already reiterating state of re-creating anew its status of emptiness, only to be filled in again by a new texture of language in the attempt to capture the resonances of the experienced real. It is an always already failed effort, but *only* in the last instance.

Traces of the experience (that is, the real) are inevitably inscribed in that atonal music produced by resonances of language that correlates with the real. The powerlessness *in the last instance* (to possess and reflect the real) is inscribed in the language re-creating the effects of the real. It can be traced in the attempts to communicate the experience in ways that are always already incomplete, doomed to repetitive acts of striving for completion. It is the desire for completion that inevitably situates thought as empty of doctrine and thirsty for the satisfaction endowed by the *lived*. The satisfaction is taken in the form of the token of this "love": the translucent texture of language, weaving around the thickness of experience.

SOLITUDE RADICALE

Radical solitude is one of the many names that Laruelle's non-philosophy gives to (the state of inhabiting) the identity in the last instance of the human-in-human, the radical concept of humanity, correlating with the real of the pure, nonreflected experience of "being human." The remnant of what cannot ever be mediated to the other (that is, transposed on the level of the transcendental) and, therefore, cannot ever enable certain deliverance from the self-enclosure (in one's "real of being") is indeed a state of radical solitude. It is the territory we have always already inhabited. And such is also the theoretical stance of thinking in terms of the real or fidelity to the real rather than to a doctrinal cosmos.

This sort of theoretical self-situating can be named non-philosophical, since it is non-philosophy that has professed it in that radical and uncompromising form I am invoking here. François Laruelle categorizes the method of non-philosophy as "scientific." What Laruelle primarily refers to when speaking of "the scientific" is its determination in the last instance, namely, the status of the authority in the last instance that the experience and experiment of the real holds (rather than acknowledging such authority as a doctrine or doxa). It is a kind of thought that situates its starting point in the object of thought and makes use of different available doctrines, creating an interdoctrinal (or interdisciplinary) assemblage of scholastic discrepancies with the sole aim of understanding the particular object of investigation.

Scientific thinking is dictated by the object of investigation, by the vicissitudes of the unpredictable real. In non-philosophy, the term "scientific" is not used in the conventional sense of the word, although it refers to an aspect of the scientific method in the conventional sense of the word; it is that aspect which differentiates scientific thought from the one Laruelle calls "philosophical." Philosophy is that vicious circle of effort toward mastering both the real and itself (the thought or the transcendental). This intrinsic, structuring component is inevitable and insurmountable for philosophy. It is its juncture of origin: the grounding division between thought and the real and the *endless dance of attempted interreflection led by the active thought vis-à-vis the dormant passivity of the real.*

Philosophy's unavoidable point of departure and its genesis consist in the decision it establishes of the relation between thinking and the real. The results of all its investigations must confirm and be in consonance with this founding decision. Non-philosophical arguing for a thought that is treated as an operation devoid of ontology, that is subjected to the real, and that issues from it as its "nonthetic reflection" and as "an absolute reflection, or without mirror"[8] is argument against divisionism. There is only one immanence and it is the same thing as the real. Thought (or "cognition," the term more frequently used in Laruelle's *Théorie des identités*)[9] operates in its territory as an occurrence of a different status (in terms of the identity in the last instance)—it is transcendental not immanent.

The argument that thought always already assumes the status of the transcendental does not imply that it has been seceded once and for all from the immanent or the real. On the contrary, non-philosophical cognition is "founded as absolute power (even though finite) upon a pure immanence, . . . exigent of the transcendence of its objects and of its representations, [and] it participates in that absolute essence or in that phenomenality entirely immanent."[10] Non-philosophical thought subjects itself to the real (*se soumet au reel*),[11] correlating with it in the attempt to reflect it nonthetically. The argument about the immediacy of thought's connection with the real is strengthened by the claim that the identity in the last instance of the subject of its mediation is an instance of the real, namely, the human-in-human (*l'homme-en-homme*). The *chôra* of the transcendental material is, in fact, "a materiality or an absolute transcendence," says Laruelle.

Evidently this claim also disturbs the classical understanding of the notions of "matter" and "materiality": "La chôra est une matérialité individuée radicalement comme matérialité."[12] So, transcendentally produced, it is the "diverse topique of and for its [thought's] distinctions,"[13] it is the "place" that is irreducibly nothing but transcendental. *Chôra* is the "place" where the transcendental "lives" in its identity in the last instance: generic and specific categories that are unorganized in a (philosophical) cosmos which dictates the meaning and the place of a category. Each transcendental product can be radicalized or reduced to its determination in the last instance, which is the correlation of the conceptual content with an instance of the real rather than the rule of a philosophical universe. There is no divisionism or dualism in non-philosophy because immanence is not split and the transcendental does not assume the position of the immanent.

Non-philosophy proposes a form of thought that is void of any pretension to (re)claiming the real. By way of abandoning its autoreferential obsession (by way of self-situating with respect to the real), thought performs a gesture of self-suspension. This is an act of self-positioning of the thinking subject that is based on the (f)actual giving way to the primacy of the real. There is no pretension of thought to controlling the real. Thought's desire to exercise absolute control over the real transposed into the phantasm of "being the real" is the origin of the founding and unavoidable split in what is called philosophical thinking. In non-philosophy, the difference between thought and the real exists only on the plane of transcendence, since the immanent is indifferent to difference.

This indifference is radical. The transcendental gravitates around the axis of the real. It is there because the real is there—it is the product of the effort of the human-in-human to mediate the "world of the real." And non-philosophy proclaims a posture of thought that has succumbed to the rule of the real and is itself an act of a Vision-in-One, and it installs this proclamation as an axiom. The operation of "seeing in terms of the one" (or the real) has an entirely different ontological (or "ontological") status, and in fact there is no ontological status in the strict sense of the word that it could inhabit; and because of this radical asymmetry, there can be neither division nor equation between them. It is something that has nothing to do with the "science of being." It is merely human practice or the practice of all beings endowed with the faculty of cognition.

The real and thought can establish neither equations nor reciprocities nor schisms of any kind, since they are not equal. Mutual equality and eventual intermirroring are impossible, because, according to non-ontology, there are no two that could establish a relation of reciprocity. There is only the one. Thinking participates in the one, that is, in the real as its "superstructure," as that translucent level of transcendence without an ontology of its own which envelops the real or the one as its instance of "autosublimation." It is the instance of interpretation, of giving meaning, of signification that dilutes the thickness of the incomprehensible real, populates it with signs, and makes it liveable through the "device" called language. The instance of thought (or of language) is the human appropriation of the real (the one). The human in its last instance or the human-in-human is (the) real and the inexorably one.

The one, as already said, is neither totalizing nor total. Rather, it is the minimal, the densest and irreducible quantity of the radical (or of pure immanence). It is not the universalizing one in the sense of the reductivist idea of a unity of differences either. It is the unique and solitary one. The real has *always already* found itself in an irredeemable solitude vis-à-vis the world (transcendence, language, thought, and mediation) and vis-à-vis the other (mediated through the world). Thinking in terms of the real and the one as the point of departure and as a point of gravitation implies universalistic gestures of thought. However, they are not universalistic in a sense that would be criticized by historicists: they are not gestures of a universalizing unity of differences but rather concurrently contingent ones. They are universal in the sense of their creation of unique language-universes (as in Laruelle) and truths embodying the desire to be valid for everyone (that is, universally).

If we accept the claim of the postmodern appropriations of the Lacanian real as the unthinkable, as the untouchable by thought (also in the sense of "not to be touched"), we are in fact claiming its factual rule over thought, since this sort of claim resides upon the premise about thought's unmitigated helplessness and detachment with respect to the real. The radical disabling of any validity of the "universe of thought" with respect to the "universe of the real" speaks of our irreparable helplessness in the face of the absolute power of the real. Laruelle's (and Badiou's in a variation of its own) arguing for thinking in terms of the real, whereby the thought suspends its pretension to authority over the real and merely *correlates* with it, opens the possibility of thought's communicating with and of the real. This is an *always already* failed undertaking, but only in the last instance. It is a failure of the attempt to grasp the real in its totality and without a remnant. However, on the level of an expectation that allows the incompleteness of the attempt of knowing the real, on the level of mediation or of communicability that is not total, the assumed stance of correlation produces degrees and forms of the real's emplacement in and for the "world."

By having recourse to an inventive use of the available doctrinal material, the non-philosophical or the radical stance of thinking in accordance with the dictate of the illogical, unpredictable, uncontrollable real also entails producing new conceptual devices (issuing in new doctrines). However, the creation of new conceptual tools or doctrines is not the primary goal. Instead, it is a posture of thought in a state of fidelity to the task of understanding a singular reality that is solitary in its radicality, a certain identity in the last instance (just as it is the case with the motivation and the ways of scientific thinking).

I would like to propose here a way of seeing the question of the relation between the real and thought or language, that is, between the human-in-human and the other or the world, as a question of love. The need to exit the real of one's radical situatedness in oneself, namely, one's situatedness in the last instance, is an act of love, an act of attempting to reach out to the other as the instance of salvation from one's radical self-enclosure. The inevitable need of the real to be mediated (for the other and the world) is something that implies the need of everyone in his or her identity in the last instance, which is the real (of his or her) being for and through the other. The attempt to speak of the love of the real will also be an attempt to speak of love.

This double attempt automatically bifurcates into two different and parallel series of questions. The first one aims to investigate the possibility of thinking love in some mode of nostalgic craving for the impossible, one ensuing from the instance of the human-in-human (*l'homme-en-homme*) as the real, the irrevocable and inconsolable one as the instance of radical solitude. The second is a series of questions interrogating the possibility of conceiving of what love might be in its own radical identity, in its identity in the last instance.

How are we to think love in the light—or the gloom—of its essential impossibility, as a form of impossibility itself, as an undertaking with an inborn autoabortion? I will attempt to situate my vision of this question in the way proffered by Laruelle under the name of a Vision-in-One. I will conform my account to the unpredictable dictate of the experience of radical solitude and produce a posture of thought in fidelity to the singularity of that experience. To put it differently, I will allow my narrative to succumb to the dictate of the real or the event, "the taking place" of radical isolation. It can be a re-creation of an event stored and operating on the level of memory (that is, internally) or an event taking place as an exteriority, a radical solitude installed by the relentless absence—death—of a loved one and continuously experienced as an inescapable state. The reference to the necessary "re-creation" of the event should only remind us that the non-philosophical posture of thought reproduces its "object" of (scientific) investigation with the unavoidable presence of the "theoretical-technical-experimental ingredients."[14] We are dealing with the instance of the "the mixed" (in the Laruellian sense: "the mixed" established by the real and thought) but without philosophical amphibology: the theorizing subject affirms the difference in status between the object of thought (correlating with the real) and the real of the object in such way that the former is recognized as transcendental and the latter as immanent.

My initial claim about love as the compulsory mode of being for the real is the following: radical solitude (the situation of the real) radically urges itself to be mediated through interventions of transcendence, that is, through language or truth. And it always already is. This bridge of mediation builds the stage for various inventions and reinventions of love in and for the "world" (in the Laruellian sense of the word), namely, that experience known to all of us which appears in a number of predetermined forms that we are all competent in (for a more or less achieved rendition of them or through failing in some of these forms of loving experience). The process of relentless autoimposed mediation of the real is the all-supporting and all-generating wheel of the experience of love contained in the various perceptions and conceptions, ideas and idealisms (of love). (It is "auto-" because there is no one and nothing but the one to impose.)

Laruelle invents the theoretical construct of the "Stranger" (*l'Étranger*) to explain the becoming of the "world" and of the "person" of and for the "world" (that is, person-in-person) as the result of the necessary process of autoalienation of the human-in-human, namely, of the self in its real. The workings of the plane of the Stranger vis-à-vis the real (or the ego in the "nonanalytical"[15] sense of the word) are elaborated in much detail in Laruelle's *Théorie des Étrangers* (1995) and *Ethique de l'Étranger* (2000). The central argument of this theory is that the human-in-human (that is, the real) is necessarily alienated (to itself) through the instance of the Stranger. My free and perhaps oversimplifying interpretation of Laruelle's theory of the Stranger, which attempts to extract its core point, is the following: in order to be able to receive, produce, and process the "world," the real makes use of its own superstructure, that is, of the instance of autoalienation or the Stranger. (The Stranger comprises the existing and potential transcendental material, and its Lacanian analogy is the language.) The repetitive act of further autoalienation is autoinstalled through the metastructure called the subject. (It is "meta-" with regard to both the Stranger and the real.)

The distinction between the real and the Stranger (and thus the world) is not to be considered as a division, as a split constituting a fundamental duality, since the difference between them is unilaterally established. The act of "unilateralization" (*unilatéralisation*) is an act of a nonrelative and nonrelationalist establishing of a relation of difference. This is an act of a singularity made of singularity, a radically solitary act of unilateral self-differentiation.[16] The concept of unilateralization can be understood through a reappropriation of the notion of unilateral difference invoked by Deleuze in *Difference and Repetition* and through resorting to the language used in this work as a rather adequate translation of the Laruellian account of the same theme. The mode of unilateral differentiation and the generic claim of the one are the two theoretical gestures that render non-philosophy a thought in terms of—or rather, in correlation with—the real and radically non-dichotomous. It is immanent to the procedure of "dualysis" (*dualyse*), which consists in the radical affirmation of the transcendental and the real as duality without scission and without unification, a duality in which each of the terms correlates unilaterally with the other.[17]

Nonetheless, emphasis should be placed on, according to Laruelle, the gesture of unilateral differentiation that pertains to the instance of the Stranger and subject, whereas the real not only remains indifferent to it but also is deprived of the possibility of performing such or any kind of gesture. The real is immanently indifferent to the relation of difference established by the act of unilateralization (or dualysis). And vice versa: the transcendental, which is always already unilaterally produced, remains radically indifferent to the *relation of indifference* of the real, which it also is to the *difference* that it might *re-present* to it (which is something that may be implicated by the position of indifference itself). Nonetheless, it is not indifferent to the effects of the real with which it correlates.

Let us now look at the possibility of conceiving of the imprints, the motions, and the commotions of the experiences of love as an instance that is unavoidably imagined, idealized, and always already engaged in the "world." Let us take a look at it on the territory proper of the experiential—the unreflected lived (Laruelle: *vécu*) of the human-in-human. Let us investigate the possibility of re-creating the traces of love—which is both a linguistic and an experiential category—inscribed on the flesh of the purely experiential (*le vécu*), that is to say, the real. If we bear in mind Laruelle's unequivocal insisting on the real's radical indifference to linguistic operations as something that takes place in and for the "world," this proposition may sound somewhat unorthodox (with respect to non-philosophy).

However, I will argue that even in the context of Laruelle's non-standard philosophy, this possibility is not so rigidly excluded, since the "communication" between the real and the Stranger is not severed. The Stranger correlates with the real. This correlation establishes a territory where the two instances necessarily meet: the lived (*le vécu*), which is also termed as "le joui" (the enjoyed) of the "jouissance" that comes from the "world." The terms belong to Laruelle's theory of nonanalysis (or "nonpsychoanalysis"),[18] which is a non-philosophical reappropriation of Lacanian psychoanalysis (most richly elaborated in Laruelle's *Théorie des Étrangers* from 1995).[19]

The imaginary approximation of this territory I find in Luce Irigaray's hiatus within the Symbolic, in the fecund muteness scarring the language and in the proximity of language to the body. I find it in her idea about the fluidity of the body, the "material" unavoidably marked by meaning, that dims "materiality" of our flesh that relentlessly emanates signification which is not easily decipherable. This body populated by the Imaginary and traversed by language is not the result of a one-sided action (that of the active subject or the language vis-à-vis the "passive" body) in the way that Judith Butler proposes to see its "imaginarization" (which is a *démarche* of ascribing sovereign authority to language with respect to the body subject to signification). It is also an active cocreator of signification, a contributing instance on the level of language, bursting with effort to translate its vibrating life, its fluctuations of both rise and fall, into an articulated expression, into a form of autosublimation.

This does not, of course, imply that the body acts as a form of a parallel "agency," performing "on its own" the gestures of autotranslation (of the body into language); but it does imply that the "I" is urged to translate its bodily experiences into language, that the urges of the body cut into the language and shape it. This theory of Irigaray that attempts to speak with "the voice of the body" can be complemented with Rosi Braidotti's "materialism of becoming." The latter is a theory that not only builds on Irigaray but also is a qualitative leap into something new that takes Irigaray's understanding of the sexual (bodily) difference as formative of subjectivity further, namely, toward the creation of a meticulously elaborated discourse called the "materialism of becoming." It is a theoretical construct drawing to a large extent on Deleuze. Braidotti's materialism of becoming does not occlude the unpredictability of the never totally conceivable body (and, subsequently, sexual difference) by way of relegating its elusive remnants (its "unthinkable") to the beyond of the real.

Braidotti sets the methodological route of theorizing the body qua body, that is, with its disturbing overtones of the real situated beyond conceivable life. In *Metamorphoses*,[20] she undertakes the laborious project of articulating the role of the unarticulated in the act of intellectual articulation par excellence—the production of a theory: "The 'feminine' for Irigaray is neither one essentialized entity, nor an immediately accessible one: it is rather a virtual reality, in the sense that it is the effect of a project, a political and conceptual project of transcending the traditional ('Molar') subject-position of Woman as Other of the Same, so as to express the other of the Other. *This transcendence, however, occurs through the flesh, in embodied locations and not in a flight away from them.*"[21]

Braidotti's understanding of gendered identity (or rather, the identity and subjectivity of the "Woman") is that it is a "project" of becoming by way of "transcending the traditional ('Molar') subject-position of Woman as Other of the Same." Her understanding is materialist: the becoming takes place through the flesh. The "materialism of becoming" is a mode of thinking, a process of continuous re-creation of conceptual apparatuses that takes into account the "occurrence through the flesh" of all transcendence. Braidotti maps the cartography of the u-topos, the "nowhere land" originally imagined and put into theoretical play by Irigaray. This image of self-situating in one's own body on the very border of the real (the ungraspable materiality of the body) while the existing (that is, the intelligible and communicable) signifiers (the symbolic) are suspended echoes Laruelle's thinking in terms of radical concepts or in accordance with the identity in the last instance. In other words, it resonates the state of radical solitude.

Radical solitude is the effect—or rather, the "mathematical principle" of "radical oneness"—of our own self-envelopment brought about by the inescapable status of the real that every human-in-human is subject to. We were all "born"—as an "I," as that most primitive sense of selfhood—in the most immediate experience of the state of inescapable situatedness in ourselves. This primacy is not temporal. It is radical. The experience of radical solitude is the most direct communication with the real (we all are) in its impossibility in the last instance to be encompassed by thought. This is a transcendentally constitutive yet radically immanent procedure of autoimposition of the act of reflection, an automatic transposition to the level of the transcendental that still remains at the heart of the nonreflected and nonreflectable. Evidently, this is a situating at the limit where the self's radical immanence initiates the primary gesture of reflection.

Therefore, the possibility of reflection is conceived in the very nebula of the nonreflectable, namely, the experience of our own real. Furthermore, what is contained as conceptual material in this two-fold—yet unilaterally engendered—situation is the (experiential) knowledge of the state of radical solitude. Hence, we can assume that all further mediation of the real—which means all reflection and transcendence—is enabled by and originates from the experience of radical solitude. The experience of love and of all of its transcendental configurations finds itself at the very origin of all and any transcendence, at the heart of the creation of all of our world(s).

LOVE AT THE HEART OF RADICAL SOLITUDE

All mediation of the real is an act of attempting to surpass and console the real's radically solitary character. In this sense, we can agree with Plato: philosophy is truly about love, and not only philosophy, but also all transcendental creation, any and all results of the activity of the linguistic agency. Love's identity in the last instance is that *always already* ultimately failed striving to surpass our indestructible—except by the advent of death—enclosure in ourselves, our own unbeatable real, to surpass and be relieved from our radical solitude(s). This initial gesture propagates into all further transcendental elaboration, into the myriad of (philosophical) translations into and for the "world."

The act of its own autotranscendence is thus immanent to the real, or rather to the woman-in-woman and man-in man as the real. Transcendence is, therefore, engendered within and by the essentially nontranscendental. And initially, it is an act of love since love is a tendency to overcome the self-enclosure of our radical immanence and introduce a fissure into the state of radical solitude. Consequently, the self-dissolution of radical solitude into an opening to the other or the "world" is radically immanent (to the real). The craving for the impossible is inherent in the radical experience of that very impossibility. The deepest yearning for the other is carved by its very own impossibility. The opening (to the other) is born on the very grounds of the ultimate self-enclosure; and conversely, the ultimate enclosure is *always already* marked by the opening for an escape to the other. The always already (the repetitiveness) plays the role of a temporal utopia, of a certain temporal presupposition that, however, implies timelessness (similar to the Bergsonian-Deleuzian concept of the duration).

The future (the becoming) is a returning past. The inborn craving for the other always already marking the real works as a *memory of a once upon a time accomplished unity* with the other. That is why any amorous yearning bears an aspect of *nostalgic* craving (which has given rise to so many myths about the original unity with the other, such as the one ascribed to Aristophanes by Plato). Nostalgia is a memory made of the inconsolable longing for the lost loved one; every loved one is always already lost. Resorting to Braidotti's "materialism of becoming," which draws, among the other Deleuzian ideas, on the Bergsonian-Deleuzian concept of becoming, we can say that the real is in an unstoppable process of a continuous, relentless autotranscendence, which overcomes its own radical solitude. Or, it is the instance of the endless circular movement of assertion of "the potency of expression," which is "about the transcendence of the linguistic signifier."[22]

We will resort to the method of unilateralization (or dualysis, which is provided by the Vision-in-One), suspending the reason of relationism (and dualism) in order to see (to establish a "theoria of") the event of (the real's) craving for (an escape to) the other in its singularity. We are faced (or we are able to produce the image of being faced) with the actuality of the act of craving, regardless of the response of the "one craved for." This impossible yearning is an actuality of a particular desire, which produces acts of imaginarization (and, thus, self-imaginarization, turning the brute physicality of desire into signification), and thus constitutes an accomplished reality in itself. The castrating impossibility imposed from the outside by the other is a positive reality entering the constitution of the castrated reality (of the "impossible" craving). The real's self-translation into that bridging reach toward the other and the "world" does not *cut* into its own self with dualism, does not thrust a division within itself, since the vision of duality (and of the consequent impossibility) belongs to the thought, not to the real. In spite of the split within thought that has been produced by the vision of the inconsolably asymmetric duality, the real inescapably reiterates its desire to transcend the state of radical solitude. In this sense, it remains radically untouched by the happenings that take place on the level of thought. Its desire to transform the grip of radical solitude into a bridge of transcendence through the other is unilaterally reaffirmed in spite of the asymmetric "response."

And this is not a paradoxical claim. Paradox is something that takes place only in terms of relation. Thinking in terms of singularity brings about something else: a self-enclosed unilaterality in a state of unstoppable reiteration. Seen from a position that belongs to the Vision-in-One, what might be an effect of paradox becomes a unilateral force of desire's self-feeding with itself. Seen in their aspect of unilaterality, these workings of our status and state of radical solitude are constituted as myriads of unique, radically solitary gestures of ultimately nonreflected experience reproducing themselves as disunited instances of the "operational" real. In other words, as an experiential stance, the self-transcending move of the real (of our own radical immanence) imposes itself as a real in its own right, as yet another instance of the nonreflected experiential that we decide to see in its singularity.

TO BE LOVED IN ONE'S OWN RADICAL SOLITUDE

Can we love (establish a "relation of fidelity to" and "produce a truth of") the other in her or his (or its) radical solitude, in her or his (or its) unmediated singularity and uniqueness while all relationism and expectation of reciprocity is suspended? Can we love the other seen in her or his (or its) resistance to the bridging of her or his (or its) radically solitary self-encompassment? Another way of putting the question would be: can we establish a relation to the other that is not relation-ist? Can we love (or establish a relation of fidelity generating truth) in a radically unilateral way? Can we relate to the other as if correlating with the real? Clearly, the medium of this operation would be the language: we are dealing with a desire that is necessarily mediated through the creations of the world (that is, the "transcendental materials" made of language). We are compelled to presuppose (or imagine or imagine a narrative of) an unavoidable recourse to the transcendental material in the process of this desire's actualization, since it is the constitutive property of thought and love inasmuch as it is that engendering gesture of all transcendence.

Departing from my declared espousal of the non-philosophical call upon thinking in correlation with the real, I would like to propose considering the possibility of conceiving of a love of the other's radical solitude (that is to say, of the real) and in correlation with the real. Therefore, what I am proposing more specifically is to conceive of a thought that takes into account—that is, that situates itself self-reflexively with respect to the imagined of—its engenderment within the desire for self-transcendence (through and to the other) while mobilizing the "imaginary infrastructure" provided by (the imagined of the other's) radical solitude.

Clearly, what can be imagined is only the imaginable itself. In other words, one can imagine only radical solitude's situation in the world, one that has been embodied by a body "populated" with significations and by an "I." One can imagine only that estranged woman-in-woman and man-in-man (imaginary, linguistic, and transcendental creations) that can only be found in the "world." The activation of thought about or introducing the stance of love toward an embodied radical solitude immanently implies the operation of the instance and the faculty of signification, that is to say, the language. Namely, one can imagine only the radical separatedness, the inconsolable solitude of the other in the world (or her or his [or its] "radical insufficiency," in Laruelle's words), together with helplessness and vulnerability intrinsic to this position. I am arguing for the possibility of establishing a relation of empathy— or of the "compassion" Laruelle writes about in his *Théorie generale des victimes* from 2012[23]—with such a transcendental rendition of the other's otherness, one based on the inceptive gesture of reaching out to the other by means of enacting solidarity with her or his (or its) imagined radical solitude and insurmountable singularity. This gesture is of a hybrid character, moulded out of both reflection, namely, the transcendental or the cognitive, and the nonreflected experiential. Empathy with the radical solitude of the other by way of identifying one's own enacted state of radical solitude with that of the (imagined) other is an *act* made both of the event of "having lived through" (*le vécu*) and of the event of the mediation provided by language (or the transcendental).

This exercise of solidarity also extends to the level of that infinite craving that takes the form of inconsolable nostalgia. The other's radical solitude necessarily intimating the impossibility of autotranscendence for him or her (or it)—as that inescapable, self-enclosed real—is what is imagined in this process. The enacted experience of nostalgia, of an empathic entering into the state of impossible craving (in the name of establishing solidarity with the other's radical solitude), is the instance at which the real (or the radical solitude) enters the play that is *in its last instance* transcendental. It is the alien body at the heart of the unstoppable processes of (self-)alienation: the transcendental production (or truth generation). The thought (which is in its last instance transcendental) correlating with the real has been invaded by a presence that is in its last instance of a radically different status: that of the real or the radical determination in the last instance.

Yet, this invasion does not stop the process of autopropagation of the estranging instance of the transcendental. The self-alienation of the human-in-human, as Laruelle puts it, or of life-in-life cannot be escaped: mediation is the only possible route of interplay between two instances of the real (both the site of the imagining subject and the site of the imagined). The transcendental is the only topos where two identities in the last instance can meet and interact, that is to say, always already through a medium, always already establishing a mediated contact. Thus, nostalgia as the defining aspect of the radical loving yearning is not only grief over one's own unbeatable radical solitude, but also mourning for the always already lost other in the immediacy of her or his (or its) nonalienated real.

The experiential encapsulation nesting in the inception of the act of radical love is "then" or "simultaneously" translated into a mediation of the imagined and identified with a radical identity. The object of our investigation received through the Vision-in-One is, in fact, that hybrid of self-enclosed subjectivity inescapably situated as a Stranger in the world. The inceptively pure and puristic move of radical solidarity will inevitably be intercepted by language. It will then be translated into the bordering level of conversion of language into solidarity with *the linguistically conceivable* identity in the last instance of the other. Namely, what is imagined, identified, and solidarized with is the identity in the last instance of the estranged for and in the world woman-in-woman (or man-in-man or "life-in-life"). One establishes solidarity with her or his (or its) determining idiosyncrasies (contingencies that are by definition the result of the impact of the real) and their solitary uniqueness (the instance of radical solitude, that is, of the real once again).

Thinking or loving one's radical solitude is a position that is also immanently radical according to its origin and according to its site of operation: in the last instance, it is determined by the radical solitude of the lover (and not only of the loved one). The bridging of solidarity with the estranged identity in the last instance arises as the result of a sense and state of unbeatable separation from the desired one (in his or her [or its] radical solitude or the real).

This radical attempt to connect with the other (in her or his [or its] real) is made of the experience of an always already frustrated interconnecting with the radical immanence of the beloved idiosyncrasies. It is an experience of witnessing the infinite retreat in self-envelopment of those ungraspable emanations of the real of the loved one, of the finite irreplaceableness of these contingencies.

THE QUESTION OF UNIVERSALISM REVISITED: THE UNIVERSAL AS RADICALLY SOLITARY POSITION

This short meditation undoubtedly resonates with what can be identified as universalistic overtones. And here we are again, returning to the question of universalism. To reiterate my already embraced position: concurring with François Laruelle and Alain Badiou, I will reaffirm my belief that every thought is immanently universalistic since the pretension to universality is constitutively inbuilt in the desire of thought. This pretension is unavoidable, as is the naïve or prelingual compulsion in every thinking endeavor to attain "the most accurate truth," "the most truthful truth"—that is to say, the Truth—of an event or of the world. This naïve compulsion is what gives birth to thought, and it is certainly prior to any self-reflection, to any autoreferential self-correctives of the thinking process that introduce criticality and political responsibility into itself. The megalomaniac positioning is immanent to thought. It is generative of its desire and it is unavoidably and radically lonely. In that ultimately fragile, vulnerable, and weak position of the fantasized omnipotence of universality, one is radically solitary.

The thought is alone facing its own desire for (or fantasy of) the ultimate truth as it is for the impossible immediacy of the other's real.

This primitive universalism—which I claim to be unavoidably present in any desiring (of thought)—is therefore radically solitary, creating a self-enclosed universe of its own. This does not mean that the thought of the world, versed in the rules and vicissitudes of the transcendental (the "Rule of History," among others), should succumb to this primitiveness and forget what it knows of the "world of difference," of the multiple faces of the world and history and of the position of criticality that history dictates.

Saying the same in a somewhat different language, I will reaffirm my position that *these* claims of universalism do not exclude the self-awareness of the thinking subject (or agency) about her or his constitutive entanglement with the social, cultural, and political context and historical background of the available transcendental material. These two presuppositions holding the status of grounding beliefs (or, for that matter, axioms) for the discursiveness deployed here do not need to be regarded as contradicting or as colliding within the same argumentation. I am assigning them a fundamentally different non-standard ontological status: the universalistic gesture of thought occupies the most primitive territory, the one spreading at the limit of language (or at the edge of Badiou's "void"), whereas the critical position in-formed by history is a purely linguistic product, an immanent product of the immanently linguistic.

Put in Badiou's terms, the thinking subject necessarily establishes a relation of fidelity to an event that is in itself (inasmuch as it is the sheer eventual or experiential) a void amid language, the unutterable as the very tissue of the immanently experiential. However, this void is at the heart of a situation that can only be linguistically conceived and that established a truth "through an endless sequence of investigations." Thus, the emergence of a new truth is the fruit of linguistic labor. Around the prelinguistic, around the void of the unrepeatable *experience*, one reinvents the language. Fidelity to an event is what reemerges as the truth process or as a generic procedure[24] establishing a certain generic subset. According to Badiou, truth does not have an ontological status per se. Nevertheless, its being can be described by mathematics. Still, "the truth is true only for its subjects, not for the spectators."[25]

This double awareness is at play in the efforts present in this text and consists in the protecting of the process of theoretical production from the arrogance of a totalitarian move of universalization. In other words, it provides us with the vigilance of theoretical responsibility for the simultaneous work of the two parallel tendencies and desires: the universalistic pretension of the singular subject and the historic accountability for the transcendental material at use. This state of vigilance, of that at least double (and potentially multiple) awareness, is once again a position of radical solitude.

A POST SCRIPTUM: POST MORTEM (TO MY FATHER)

The experience of the loss of a loved one is complex and comprises many intersecting layers of heterogeneous origin: some of them are of linguistic provenance and character, others are of the purely nonreflected experiential. The latter consist of sheer pain, suffering made of ache, throbbing resulting from the simple experience of being severed from the loved one, regardless of our convictions about and beliefs and interpretations of the "nature" of (any) connection with and attachment to the other: whether one claims its always already imaginary, phantasmatic, linguistically mediated character or insists on its specific substance (inasmuch as it is essence), the experience of grieving itself is that of pure suffering inflicted by the sensation of being severed from the loved one. Even for a psyche submerged in fantasies (convictions) about the purely phantasmatic character of its relation (of love) with the lost loved one, the state of grief is—primarily or constitutively— made of the nonreflected, the ultimately evasive to any reflection experiential of sheer pain.

The irrevocable—radical—parting with the (phantasmatic or "in the real") loved one can only take place in the purely experiential (or in the event of death or the radical loss of a loved one, prior to any reflection or truth generation), that is to say, in the real. The irrevocability of the parting in the real is sensed as the denuded real, stripped of any meaning, of any significance that "will make sense." The very event and instance—as a state "of being," of "existence," an ontological status of "being in the real"—of irrevocability is only the presentification of the real in its absolute form, cleansed from the soothing, that is, *estranging*, workings of the world. It is the sheer thrust of the absurd, beyond language. It is the brutal and senseless trauma brought about by and as the real.

The real of grieving is conditioned and defined by its attachment to a unique, unrepeatable event of an irreplaceable singularity of a person, by the fact that the mourning and longing for the lost loved one is only mourning for that particular person. One inconsolably mourns the loss of a concrete person. That particular and concrete person is a "particular one" and "concrete" because he (or she) is that singular and unique human-in-human, entrapped in his (or her) own now dissolved real. The concrete person is concrete because he (or she) has always and inescapably been that concrete human-in-human or that real (of a person), who has always escaped into estrangement as a Stranger to our always already failed attempts to grasp him (or her) in his (or her) real.

The brutality of the trauma of severance in the real can hurt and wound; it can lastingly bring pain only when cloned (as Laruelle says) from a sample of the realities of the world. The numb, organic experience of pure pain brought about by the radical severance from the loved one survives only if planted upon a phantasm, interbreeding with a signification (a memory that gives rise to a state of nostalgia, endless desire for endless repetition of gestures loaded with a certain meaning). The absurd real beyond thought—both in savored closeness as well as in severance from the loved one—is kept alive by its interface with thought (through sentimental phantasms or remembering phantasms, that is to say, *memory*) by its acts of cloning with the language.

And in grieving and longing for the lost loved one, in mourning where the sensation of pure pain is predominant in composition vis-à-vis the soothing elements of estrangement (the workings of reflection, the transcendental), the phantasm is colored, invaded by the sensation of the brutal absurdity of the real. Remembrance (remembering old and new phantasms of desire, of love) is projected by the dark, thick sensation of the real of love and the real of loss. The event of longing for this (even if and even though fantasized, imaginary, or symbolic) loved one (*in-dividual*) is real: it is in the real.

And the dark, thundering real of this love invades and colors in black the brilliant remembrances of love—and what takes rise is a sheer shriek of hurt. The blackness and the luminosity, the absence of color in the singularity of pain and the radiant colorfulness of craving memories, begin to merge, to create a fusion that will be the gloomy point of genesis of new light and color. A nostalgic song of love will begin to compete with the shriek of ache, in a dolorous yet hopeful struggle to replace it. Put another way, the real (of the sheer trauma) and the thought (of the world of language) are the coagulating elements of this emerging brilliance of renewed desire for the other—of the love born anew.

5

THE REAL IN THE IDENTITY

THINKING IN FIDELITY TO THE REAL
(BEHIND THE IDENTITY)

How are we to think our situatedness within an identity, such as that of a "woman" (or any other identitary subjection) while observing one of the main principles of François Laruelle's non-philosophy, situating the thought in correlation with the real? Or, to rephrase the question, how can we think the problems of identitary subjection while escaping the vicious circle of the philosophy thinking itself? Namely, conceptualization in relation to another conceptualization, detached from the reality of what is subject to the particular process of generating truth. How can we produce truths that establish a relation of fidelity to the reality that is being questioned by way of stepping out of the enclosure of the philosophical self-mirroring?

Or rather, how can we proceed with the act of theorizing a particular sample, a particular cut of our social-cultural reality that is an identity in which we inescapably always already find ourselves, without falling into the trap of becoming accomplices in the perennial play of philosophy's autoreferential self-legitimization? In other words, how can we theorize by way of drawing legitimacy in the last instance for our insights not from the doctrinal compounds made of transcendental material but from the authority of the real?

The non-philosophy of Laruelle engages into a project of establishing theoretical grounds for a thinking that can escape the impasse of "specularization," of autoreflexivity and autolegitimization as the defining constituent of philosophy. And the unavoidable route of accomplishing this, according to non-philosophy, is establishing a unilaterally situated thought. This involves a cognitive posture devoid of any relationism produced by and situated within the doctrinal horizon(s), producing a thought of singularity that only unilaterally correlates with the real. I shall attempt to make use of this Laruellian proposition for the purposes of creating a thinking stance that is faithful in the last instance to the reality of the *lived* identitary subjection. It will also be faithful to the reality of the transcendental identitary frame (the identity subjugation as prescribed by the world) acting in such a compelling way upon the real ([of] the human-in-human) that it itself acts as an instance of the real.

Since my trajectory of thought here is evidently establishing a relation of attuning with the ruling overtones of the non-philosophical voicing(s) of Laruelle, it is important to note that the language I employ is not in a seamless correspondence with that of non-standard philosophy. On the contrary, it deviates at some important points, and in reference to some key notions in the discussion. Non-philosophy calls what is in this text and otherwise known as identity or identitary subjection "the Stranger." Identity, in the vocabulary of non-philosophy, is always "identity in the last instance," namely, the real.

This reality—the identity that we seek to understand and generate certain truth of—belongs to the world and it has been made of the transcendental. It is a discursive, purely conceptual product(ion)— and an action, the living reality of the transcendental—that takes place in, by way of, and for the world. Yet it is lived and ruled by the unruly real (or by a particular unruly real). Thus, the attempt is to engage in a process of truth-production whereby the ultimate source of legitimacy, the arbiter in the last instance, is the unique, lived reality of the subject of our quest for understanding, and not the adept observance of the laws of interplay of transcendental accomplishments (philosophical discourses).

This is an attempt to be accountable to what is not accountable to the transcendental: the reality of the lived identitary subjection that always already escapes the pretension of language to encompassing it and fixing it by turning it into a meaning. Even if our task were to understand and explain the laws in the reality of identitary subjection that evade assigned meanings and possibilities of interpretation, this limit should not be suppressed but rather should become the source of a new language. Or, in Badiousian parlance, the voice or the clamor of the "evental site" should become the stage of a new language. Most probably, the emerging language will initially be in utter dissonance with the linguistically available materials and disturb all discourses that make sense. On the transcendental plane, this new and singular truth will be something that does not make sense, whereas on the level of the event (of an "unheard of reality"), it will have an explanatory power, initially recognizable perhaps only to those who inhabit the evental site.[1]

A theoretical undertaking of this kind should consist in escaping the (philosophical) mode of thinking in which the philosophical decision is the arbiter in the last instance over the reality at stake, that is to say, the identity as ruled by the real. Decisionism—as to what the or a reality is about—is that which is identified by Laruelle as the very origin of philosophical self-sufficiency and specularization, a process in which one (speculative) decision draws legitimacy from another. Philosophy legitimizes philosophy. This is a process of narcissistic mirroring in which philosophy makes claims over what is extraneous to it, over the or a reality it seeks to explain, that is, to establish a truth of.[2] Such an act of thought takes place in a way that implies discounting the real ruling the or a reality in its uncontrollable and ungraspable ways, inasmuch as it is the unthinkable aspect of any reality, while appropriating that same reality (of the identity in question) solely according to the rules of its governing decision.

Thus, together with the gesture of establishing an immaculately conceptual possession over the or a reality, the philosophical thought also performs an infantile act of engulfing the lump of the real that is dispossessed (of any authority). This is precisely "the relation of the mixed" (*le rapport de mixte*), the "amphibological reality," or the "limitrophy of the real" in which, according to Laruelle, the philosophical generation of truth comprises that which the non-philosophy strives to surpass—or rather, bypass—by thinking in *correlation with* the real: its self-sufficiency.

The relational interconditioning of concepts is that which necessarily brings thought to the state and status of unity of (reconciled) contrarieties. It totalizes it and renders it unitary (by way of performing unification into an orderly whole, a cosmos). (Even when the tension is seemingly preserved through the relation of opposition or paradox between contrarieties that participate in the "orderly whole," what in fact takes place is their "reconciliation" by way of transforming them into accomplices in the accomplishment of some cosmos.) And only to remind ourselves of what has been at length explicated in the previous chapters of this book, the unity (in the sense of an accomplished whole, cosmos, structure, organism, and so on, but *not* in the sense of an affirmed oneness as singularity) is always already dualistic, synthesizing the two or leaving them *in a relation* of split (which still holds them together).[3] Thought's correlation with the real is an instance of its unilateral situating with respect to the real, whereas the real "responds" to this act of unilateralization with a "nonresponse." Namely, it remains in the last instance indifferent to it. In fact, and to be more precise, the act of unilateralization or "dualysis" is characterized by an indifference in the last instance vis-à-vis the response of the other.

In such a theoretical undertaking, which does not answer, in the ultimate instance, to any doctrine, but to the investigated reality and to its identity in the last instance, which is the elusive real (participating in that reality in a way that is deciding), one faces, yet again, the necessity to operate, but to do so with the transcendental. Thinking operates with what is immanent to it and, more importantly, with that over which it can claim authority, namely, with the realm of thought, with concepts or language, with conceptual-linguistic structures or compounds and their intrinsic modes of generation and operation. Notwithstanding, thought can decide to be accountable in the last instance to the reality that has always already been assumed by the vicissitudes of the real.

Thus, the process described above gives rise to the resistance of the real to thought's aspirations to grasp it by enfolding it into a concept. The limitations that the real will impose on the pretensions of thought will be the authority in the last instance to the theoretical claims of its "nature," "essence," and so on. The limit, the occlusion of thought stemming from the absurd real, will be the instance of legitimization of a truth that immanently and inescapably strives to appropriate it by turning it into a controllable meaning. The real remains indifferent to the processes of truth generation. However, thought is affected by the workings of the real. Its arrogance is restrained and its aspirations are disciplined by the undisciplined responses of the disorderly real. At precisely these points (of resistance), thought should proffer its silence, relegate the real to its own domain, and thereof attempt to situate itself with respect to those cracks shoved into the language by that unintelligent and banal real. Those cracks will become the voices of dissonance that may give birth to an unheard of and singular appropriation of language and ultimately, perhaps, contribute to some dramatic transformation of it.

According to Laruelle's "science of the humans," put in the technical terms of this theory, one can think humanity (which is always already that of the world, made of the transcendental) in correspondence with the real only if it is taken as residual of the transcendental that has been lived by the real. "Ego" in nonanalysis[4]—the non-philosophical reappropriation of psychoanalysis—is another first name for the real.[5] Humanity, which is a transcendental category, a matter of "representation," is always already lived by the nonanalytical ego (or the real or "le moi-un," the "cause of representation"). Lived humanity, both as agency and as positive reality, is called the Stranger (*l'Étranger*).[6] Humanity is only the transcendental material (philosophy), conceptual complexes interpreting and situating the human in the world. These complexes are always already made of these very interpretations; they are the product of language, through which humanity and the Stranger are inescapably appropriated in order to be or by virtue of being "received and lived in the ego."[7]

It is important to note that, according to the non-philosophical theory of the human, namely, "the science of humans," and by way of resorting to a (re)invention of a theoretical-scientific apparatus based on the transcendental material provided by psychoanalysis termed "nonanalysis," the ego remains indifferent to all the misfortunes and fortunes of the Stranger. It is indifferent to the restructurings and repositionings, to the internal fissures and aporetic conflicts, to the reconciling and unifying moves of synthesis and dialectic resolutions. It is indifferent to all of that which belongs to and takes place on the level of representation (of humanity), that is to say, in terms of humanism.

This indifference of the nonreflected and nonreflectable real intimates the gesture of unilateral difference, which is always already performed by the Stranger (the bearer of humanism) vis-à-vis the ego, that is, the real. Yet, it lives from and is lived as the real. Thus, even if thought suffers from the ambition to define the real and to establish a relation of possession or of reciprocity of any kind, the "numbness," the radical indifference of the real, disables any relation except that of nonrelation, that is, of unilaterality.

The gesture of unilateralization is one of the key theoretical procedures applied by non-philosophy that renders thought nondualistic, that is, nondichotomous and nonoppositional and, therefore, nonunitary. The Stranger is conceived through a unilateralizing posture of thought as unilaterally positioned (vis-à-vis the real). The Vision-in-One of this dual structure is nondualistic since what is envisioned is the radical asymmetry of unilateral *ek-stasis* (*extase-sans-horizon*)[8] of the two notions. There is no relation, no reciprocity, and no pretension of thought to usurping the authority of the last instance of the human-in-human. Whatever thought might think, the real radically does "not care" and remains untouched by it. Hence, no internal fissures and no schism into the tender flesh of the utmost-intimate self have been made possible by the "science of the humans."

To sum up: to think humanity non-philosophically and to establish a (non-philosophical) science of the human that takes into account the real is something founded upon and ensured by the act of unilateralization (or "dualization"). The thought of unilateral differentiation brings forth the concept of the Stranger, of lived humanity (lived by the ego and in the real). The Stranger is estranged from the radically immanent self (the ego) dwelling principally in the territory of the transcendental. However, through his or her rootedness in and constitutive intertwining with radical immanence, the Stranger proffers a theoretical tool engendered by the residual of the transcendental that has been lived in the real. It carries the knowledge of the lived humanity (or even the lived humanism): "The experience of the human of his [or her] humanity is that of the simple transcendence, of an exteriority that does not transcend for the second time on the basis of a (re)folding over itself, which is given one-time-every-time without being regiven."[9] The sheer *experience* of humanity is, therefore, one occurring in an immediate fashion through that instance of mediation called the Stranger. It always already remains anterior to any further re-creation of the transcendental through reflection that is inevitably reflection reflecting itself.

WHO IS THE SUFFERER: THE STRANGER OR THE REAL?

> L'homme est cet Idiot qui existe aussi comme Humanité
> universelle ou Etranger.
> —Laruelle, *Théorie des Étrangers*[10]

The ego, in the nonanalytic sense, or the identity in the last instance is the human in and as that utter void of reflection—the human-in-human devoid of transcendence, the ultimate instance, that of fundamental vulnerability and irreconcilably nontranscended insufficiency.[11] It is the instance of radical solitude, an instance to which the language or the transcendental is an exteriority. Moreover, it is only through this exteriority that it can survive in the world. It is radically "insufficient only when it comes to thinking, and precisely because it is itself foreclosed to thought."[12] It is radically insufficient and vulnerable when it comes to its survival in the world.[13]

The real is clearly the instance beyond thought, beyond language, the silent, the quiet, and the quietist ego, where we all reside in the last instance. It is our radical identity. This "beyond" is not a "meta-"; it is rather a certain "epekeina" that is "over there somewhere" and that does not establish a vertical or any other pseudospatial relation with respect to the Stranger and her or his world, neither an axiological one. It inhabits an ou-topos, being a singularity that, by definition, obliterates, engulfs the space. Just like the Stranger (that is, the thought that could invent the Stranger), it is unilaterally nonrelational, nonunitary, and nondualistic. Each of the instances is seen in its radical identity, in its singularity, in its own real: in the ungraspable, elusive, and uncontrollable (by conceptualization) uniqueness of its reality. Transcendence in its aspect of experience lived by the human-in-human in the form of the Stranger, and ruled by the real urges us to consider it as yet another actuality of the real. Still, the positive reality of the Stranger, or the "substance" it is made of, or the instance it represents constitutes and is constituted by the transcendental.

Theory will *unilateralize* (or "dualize") the two instances. For the sake of establishing nondecisional, non-philosophical, nondualistic thinking, a non-philosophical theory will introduce a unilateral nonrelation of the two instances that establish the "mixed" (*le mixte*) and cohabit via the Stranger. This "mixture" will be introduced without opposing the two terms, without establishing any dichotomy. It will search for the points where the two meet, intertwine, and coproduce realities. It will attempt to "see," to think these points as singularities, that is to say, in a nonrelationist way.

In the strict sense, the real does not inhabit the Stranger. The latter is constituted only of transcendence. Yet again, transcendence comprised by and through the Stranger is always already entrenched in a (or the) real of a human(-in-human) or of life(-in-life) and reappropriated by the incongruities of a certain radical immanence.[14] Technically speaking, to say that transcendence (rendered by the Stranger) takes place in the domain of the real is a falsification of Laruelle's theory. Namely, the creator of non-philosophy insists on the indifference of the real with regard to the "humanist processes" that take place in the domain of the Stranger and in the world. Parallel to this insistence, which holds the status of an axiom in his theory, Laruelle also makes the following claim of divergence: "One should note that the Stranger is not the relation of the ego with the world, a synthetic relation of reciprocity and convertibility. It is a relation, which is relatively autonomous, extracted from the world (of the metahuman mixed), and which is received and lived in-ego and in-human without being a relation to the ego."[15]

The notion of the residual is, thus, based on the founding presupposition about the intrinsic intertwining of the transcendental and the real. And this is clearly stated in the following paragraph: "In effect, that residual cannot be constituted by the sole and pure transcendence, supposed to be empirically abstracted from the mixed, and opposed to the immanence of the ego. . . . We are not making of the ego yet another metaphysical and idealist use and are, consequently, not saying that it only implies a dissolution without any residue of the amphibology of the ego and the Xenos."[16] Still, it remains Laruelle's strong claim that the real is radically indifferent to the experiences of the Stranger.[17] The Stranger is always already "touched" (*affecté*) by the real—or rather, in the grasp of the real—whereas the real continues to be *untouched* by the concerns of the Stranger and by the world. Laruelle states clearly that "[the real] invalidates the most fundamental Greek presuppositions about 'man's place in the World,'" that it is "the end of the cosmopolitical paradigm."[18] However, this does not mean utter dissociation between the two instances and, hence, a constitutive split. Quite the contrary, through the Stranger, the radically immanent ego experiences its humanity and the world in a singular mode of its unrepeatable lived, while still remaining that disengaged instance of "a certain beyond." The dynamics are asymmetric and the two instances relate without being relationally interconstituted. They create an "interface" of a unilateral kind. The relation of the ego to humanity or to the humanist world of the real is explained in the following way: "There is also the transcendence in general, in which the ego does not engage itself, but which is engaged by it [by the ego] as 'human.'"[19] The human, according to Laruelle, rids "Being" (l'Être, which in Laruelle's theory is a philosophical concept par excellence) from its "philosophical form, . . . giving it a real, purely human essence or an identity."[20] This operation takes place in-the-ego (en-Ego) and not beginning with or issuing from the ego (non pas depuis ou à partir de l'Ego).[21] The human-in-human's experience of (her or his own) humanity is one of "a simple transcendence, of an exteriority that does not transcend for the second time on the basis of a (re)folding [(re-)pli] over itself, which is given one-time-each-time without being regiven."[22] Thus, the experience of transcendence that takes place in the real (or in the ego) also takes place as that instance of the nonreflected, preceding any autoreflexive autotranscendence of the transcendental. It is a sheer experience of the transcendental of "humanity" inasmuch as it is an exteriority that happens to the ego-in-ego and in-the-ego (and not beginning with the ego).

I would argue that through this theoretical move of enabling unilaterally initiated exchange while preserving the identity in the last instance as one of singularity, the danger of inaugurating yet another ontology (or nonontology) of a dichotomous fissure at the heart of human's genesis has been effectively avoided. Laruelle is clear—and rather exhaustive in his clarification—that all which takes place on the level of the Stranger is "processed" or lived through the real. Finally, all experience that is in its last instance nonreflected—moreover, that "represents" or constitutes the instance itself of nonreflection—is only the real. In line with this, Laruelle speaks of "le joui" of the real, taking place inside the instance of radical immanence, while issuing from—and into—*jouissance*. The territory proper of *jouissance* is transcendence since it is the creation of the instance of representation, the language.

Yet again, the radical quietism of the real with respect to the world begets the *dilemma* as to whether the real can create the possibility of putting the world into such theoretical use that this use would create another unintended dualism, in spite of the assurances against it provided by the procedure of unilateralization (or "dualization"). More specifically, I am referring to the possibility of a split use of the "explanatory infrastructure" of Laruelle's theory in spite of the thinking stance of preserving oneness at the instance of the ego or the real. In other words, Laruelle's theory offers the promise of untouched integrity for the experience of radical immanence by protecting the identity in the last instance from the philosophically produced split. And this promise is secured by the principle of thought's correlating with this oneness. However, the utter linguistic detachment of the real that is purported may infuse the use of language with a sense of the radical incapacity to embrace the desire for improving the conditions of the human-in-human in this world.

Although the real is the identity in the last instance of everything of humanist provenance that can be experienced or of all that might take place in the world (ruled by the language), it still is essentially beyond language. It is mute. Laruelle's claim is (intended as) unequivocal and is repeated in many places and ways throughout his opus: the real (of) ego possesses radical autonomy.[23] Thus, the question is: is it *essentially* linguistically incompetent? In other words, does the "idiot aspect" of the Stranger come from the irreparably and linguistically incapacitated real of the human-in-human?

Furthermore, does the defining seclusion of the real from the language not in some way imply a constitutive division at the heart of the human-in-human? Resorting to philosophical terminology, let us say that such an implication is a political rather than an ontological one. Namely, the (dis)engagement in the world that non-philosophy seems to profess may be interpreted as political defeatism, as affirmation of human's radical impotence in reshaping the world. However, such an interpretation is in direct opposition with Laruelle's idea about immanent revolt nesting in the real of every human-in-person, stemming from its radical vulnerability always already interpellated to revolt.[24]

The singularistic political stance and the revolt stemming from radical solitude enable action against singular, solitary, and unrecognized instances of oppression. Similarly, in *Ethics*, Badiou professes action against isolated, solitary instances of oppression without the necessary construction of an entire ideological universe explicating and justifying the action: "I would be delighted to see today so constant an attention paid to concrete situations, so sustained and so patient a concern for the real [*le réel*], so much time devoted to an activist inquiry into the situation of the most varied kinds of people."[25] This position enables activism related to those inhabiting the "evental site," those whose suffering is invisible and whose oppression is unintelligible through the existing forms of discursiveness.[26]

As for the question of the possible (non)ontological implication of constitutive dualism, I dismiss that possibility, since, as explicated at length in this and the previous chapters, the identity in the last instance of all world's happenings is only the real, the one-in-one, the human-in-human as radical immanence whose oneness is a unilateral matter. This is a position of inherent disabling of any possibility of philosophically inaugurating a constitutive division within the human-in-human and in the Vision-in-One of her or him or it and of her or his or its estranged self in this world.

At this point, it is important to raise the following question: if the division and the inner conflicts—the constitutive splits of human subjectivity or of the sense of selfhood—can be brought about only by the transcendental, if in the last instance they are philosophically generated, then who suffers in the last instance from the anxieties that accompany these processes? Is it the Stranger in her or his humanist aspect or is it the real (participating in that "mixture" called Stranger)?

Or rather, where does the identity in the last instance of the suffering reside? Laruelle's answer is: in the real. In fact, he explicitly states this in the elaboration of his proposition for a non-philosophical appropriation of psychoanalysis called nonanalysis. Namely, speaking of "le joui"—which belongs to the realm of the real—Laruelle says: "It is the undivided (of) pain—yet not determined by it—as the undivided lived of joy, but never their synthesis, not even immanent."[27]

Still, the question remains: If the real is indifferent to the specific properties of the Stranger (inasmuch as it is the produce of the transcendental), and if it is linguistically incompetent, how can it suffer (for) the "violence(s) of metaphysics" occurring in the world and to the Stranger? To put it differently, if the identity in the last instance of the suffering is in the real, while the real is indifferent to the transcendental in a way that is defining, then can we assume that, in Laruelle's non-philosophy, the real suffers the suffering but not what the suffering is about or what is suffered from or for?

If I am suffering from an "inflicted sense of dignity" (= transcendental) of my "identity as a woman" (= transcendental), am I really suffering from an inflicted sense of dignity or am I, in the last instance (that of the real), merely suffering the suffering or the suffered? In *Théorie des Étrangers*, we read: "The joui-that-is-nothing-but-the-joui is not the result or the product of an operation of transcendence of the *jouissance*; it is the joui-in-joui or immanent (to) itself rather than to the *jouissance* that would give or constitute it."[28] Thus, "le joui" or "the lived"—that is, the real—is given or constituted by "the jouissance," which is transcendental by its determination in the last instance and in its positive reality. Yet again, as such, as the real proper, as the "joui-which-is-noting-but-joui," it is neither the result nor the product of the "transcendent operation of *jouissance*." Resituating this paragraph within the overall framework of Laruelle's theory, we find it under the light of a theory that allows us to reread it and retell it in the following—perhaps more clarifying—way: Although the *jouissance* (or the transcendental) can— and always already does—issue in and render itself as lived experience, the "joui" as the identity in the last instance of the *lived jouissance* is produced elsewhere, namely, in its radical immanence. Therefore, the "joui," the real of and as the lived, is another autonomous occurrence—an event, a phenomenon, or, mathematically put, a separate unit or set—that has been autoproduced on one level, namely, the real, by the intervention of another, namely, the transcendental.

The two occurrences are in their last instance unilaterally generated and positioned, and, seen in their last instance (that of radical immanence), they are nonrelated and nonreciprocal. Finally, let us not forget that the unilaterality of the difference between the two instances and the in-division of the human(-in-human) is the founding principle of the non-philosophical discourse, the point of gravity of all that has been said and will be said with the language of this theoretical project.

RELAYING THE REAL TO THE ESTRANGED HUMAN

At this point, it still seems virtually impossible to locate the point, or—if it is not a question of location—to conceive of a process of immediacy of communication (or, perhaps, translation) between the two instances and the two respective genera of occurrences. Surely, what is at stake here is emphatically not a synthesis—a gesture of unification of the two components into a binary construct—but precisely the possibility of communication between the two instances. If the real in its utter muteness—which, as it happens, participates in the genesis of the Stranger—remains inalterably and implacably indifferent and impeded in relation to the concerns of the transcendental within the Stranger, a certain schismatic status is implied in the very tissue of the most immediate and most intimate, that is, radical and immanent, experiences of the human.

This absolute indifference renders any flexion and inflexion or, if nothing else, any infliction brought upon the Stranger as nothing but a hallucination for the identity in the last instance. If the real is the "topos" and the "material" of the identity in the last instance, and if it always already discounts in an absolute way the relevance of the questions tormenting the Stranger, then, one might conclude, it is irrelevant (in the last instance) if one suffers from an infliction on her or his "dignity" inasmuch as one is a woman, or gay, or black, or poor. Can one say that content of the infliction is irrelevant to the real, which is a mere receptacle of the designified suffering? And are we not unjust—that is to say, not "caring-of-the-other"—if we put it so?[29] Or, in other words, if the real bears only the "suffered" and has no bearing on what is suffered from, then the sufferings of the inflicted "dignity" of an identity have no relevance in the last instance. Finally, are we to understand that one's malaise about one's status as a woman—or gay, or black, and so on—is ultimately *immaterial* to one's identity in the last instance, which is that of the voiceless real? It is only fair to say that Laruelle's non-philosophical opus neither offers nor provides solid grounds for an explicit or unequivocal response to a question such as this one. I would like to investigate the potentiality of this discourse for creating an insight into the ways of interaction between the two instances that might accord the legitimacy of the real to the humanist anxieties of identity (that is to say, render them real).

Surely, the real, termed the ego(-in-ego), when viewed in its corelation—yet emphatically not its constitutive relatedness—with the Stranger, namely, the *lived transcendental*, is, in fact, the identity in the last instance of the Stranger. In that sense, it grounds the Stranger as the real. At this point, the crucial question is that of legitimization by the authority of the real of the positive reality of the transcendental, incorporated by or through the Stranger.

Consequently, could I say that, in the last instance, I am indifferent to the injurious subjection of my identity as a woman in the "world" (in the Laruellian sense)? Is my identity in the last instance—that "self" which lives in and as that inescapable situatedness within the real of me, which is unarticulated and irreducible to any concept(s)—entirely "illiterate" and indifferent with respect to my experiences as a woman (which is an identitary, that is, transcendental, phenomenon)? Is that "insufficient, frail" human-in-human (according to Laruelle)[30]—which I am in my identity in the last instance—so absolutely incompetent and numb with respect to my ordeals as a Stranger-woman?

The real of me is always already nontranscended and therefore irreducible to a meaning. It is that "being grasped within myself," which cannot be undone and transcended in the last instance. And this grasp can be named "the real," "the human-in-human," or the "identity in the last instance," but it cannot be a name. It is indifferent to naming in the sense that it does not need it in the last instance.[31] The real of my reality is elusive to naming and conceptualization, and it is irreducible to a meaning, since it is autochthonous and prevails according to its own inconceivable ways and in spite of the appetite of the transcendental to appropriate and tame it. In its last instance, it is essentially indifferent to the linguistic pretensions to its reappropriation.

On the other hand, if the real is not to be taken as a certain "meta-" or "idealistic" locus, if it is always already participating in the life of the Stranger (if it is "radically autonomous but not exclusive"), deprived of any potentiality to "live an independent life" in the absolute or exclusive sense, then it cannot be—in a particular instance—entirely indifferent linguistically. And the "particular instance" is that of the immediately lived exteriority of transcendence prior to its "(re-)pli sur soi," resulting in "transcendence's self-transcendence" or the narcissistic mirroring of philosophy. The non-philosophical discourse implies a constitutive entanglement of the real with the transcendental.

In other words, it allows us the possibility for a legitimate assumption about the self-generated compulsion of the real to reappear, to reestablish itself as the necessary subject to its own alienation and to transcendence. It allows the possibility for such an assumption by its disallowing of the constitutive split of the two instances, which is supplemented by these two axioms: (a) the identity in the last instance of all is the real or the one, and (b) the real is that in which and by which the transcendental humanity is *lived*. The instance of estrangement (incorporated in the Stranger) is inevitably *lived*; the identity in the last instance of every personalized estrangement, that is, of the Stranger, is the radically immanent ego or the real. If the real is the identity in the last instance of any and all reality (and thus also of those linguistically constituted), we can venture the hypothesis that it is the real that *always already* propels itself toward its own—although in the last instance impossible—transcendence. The suffocating self-enclosure of the real strives to surpass its own inescapability—through (self-) estrangement, through self-transcendence.

Thus, the generation of that "shadow"—the Stranger—is rooted in the necessity (implied by the very "character" of the real) that the identity in the last instance reproduces itself in (and for) the world. If that compulsion for estrangement originates from a certain genuine discomfort of the real (and in the minimal sense from that claustrophobic self-enclosure), then the ways of (linguistic) articulation of its alienated positioning in the world cannot be essentially arbitrary. These processes, of course, take place through the Stranger.

Even though the processes of articulation (the workings of the transcendental) are taking place on another level, through another instance which is that of the estrangement, the very need for articulation, I would argue, is begotten by the real (of that nonreflected identity in the last instance). Even though the articulation (the production of the transcendental) begins only with the establishing of the instance of estrangement (of the real from itself) and solely through it, the begetter of those (alienated) processes cannot be—in an "other than in the last instance"—utterly incompetent in relation to them. Again, this "other than in the last instance" would be the instance of the immediacy of the *lived transcendental* insofar as it is *an experienced exteriority* prior to any "(re-)pli sur soi" of the transcendence.

To conclude, in its aspect of the real, inasmuch as it is that identity in the last instance that has not been estranged, the "ego" (in nonanalytical terms) remains indifferent to the workings of identification on the level of the Stranger. Nonetheless, inasmuch as it is that constitutive—

and, moreover, concerned—ingredient within the Stranger, the real implies a certain signifying competence in its own right. If nothing else, even though the real does not speak the language of the transcendental, it can and necessarily does respond to it.

Everything that has been *lived* by the Stranger, even on that shadowy level of the "humanist human" (that is, the transcendental), finds its last instance of identity *lived*, in the real. Therefore, one can claim that the real remains indifferent to the humanistic anxieties over "who we are in this world," to those concerns and affairs that belong to the territory proper of philosophy. However, I would argue that it is always already *touched*—and moreover *concerned* and *implied*—by the "transcendental" that has been *lived through* that "idiot that we are" (according to Laruelle), the Stranger. In that sense, I will venture the claim that my malaise as a "woman" thrown into this "world" carries the grain of the discomfort of the real, and the complicity of the real rather than its indifference toward my inflicted situating in this world (or "world").

THE WORLD

In the article "L'identité sexuée," François Laruelle and Anne-Françoise Schmid argue for a "displacement of the problem of the relationship between the sexes (genders)" inasmuch as it is a binary construct of opposition endlessly re-created by the philosophies of the world (this term also includes science and religion with their philosophical tenets). Instead of being constantly and transcendentally reproduced as a given (by the world) gendered identity, they suggest the possibility of "living through one's own destiny the destiny of the world," and call upon the "faculty of giving the world to oneself" and the "sentiment of being *for* it rather than *in* it."[32]

This quotation may seem to imply a claim about the possibility of an essential detachment of the human-in-human (*l'homme-en-homme* together with his or her situation and mode as a Stranger) from the world. Arguing for a gesture of "giving the world to oneself" might resonate as an intimation about the world's utter arbitrariness and the possibility for a repetitive re-creation entirely according to the individual's volition. This way of understanding the quoted paragraph may as well be encouraged and seemingly corroborated by the call for creating a sentiment of "being *for*" rather than "*in* the world." However, such a reading of the quotation is possible and sounds plausible only if the cited words are taken out of the overall context of non-philosophy.

The entire construction of such a hypothetical reading can be undercut by the central proposition in this quotation, namely, the possibility of *living* "through one's own destiny the destiny of the world." Both this argument and the favoring of a language according to which we are "for" rather than "in" the world should be read in accordance with the more general and axiomatic presuppositions of the theory of non-philosophy, which argues for a thought that correlates with the real. Namely, it is a claim that calls upon thinking which draws its legitimacy from the solitary, vulnerable, and linguistically impeded instance of the real of our ultimate self, rather than from the existing "cosmos of discursiveness," thinking that is answerable in the last instance *to* its own lived experience *of* the world—or to the lived *through* the world as well as *in* the real—and *not to* the world itself, that is, not to the ruling discourse(s) and the concomitantly prescribed practices. One is called upon to answer to and draw legitimacy from one's own most intimate self, notably from the point at which the real, that ultimate and irretrievable situating of the utmost self, is being affected by the workings of language.

Considering that non-philosophy professes nondichotomous thinking, disallowing—from a position of an axiom—the possibility of assuming a relation of opposition and mutual exclusion between the real and the world, to understand the authors as making a claim about the essentially *illusionary* nature of the world is, if nothing else, misleading. The real possesses a "location" of its own that is neither discursive nor real, neither material nor ideal, neither ontic nor nonontic, which implies a *real* (that is, in the real) detachment from and positing beyond ("meta-") the world. The conceptual purity of the two notions should not be confusingly identified with a conceptualizing of two instances (the real and the world) as purified from each other in the real. The purity of the concept is a theoretical reality, and it does not imply a claim to the real or—perhaps it is more accurate to say—about the reality that originates and lives from the intertwining of the real and the world.

Within this particular theoretical horizon, the only topological situating of the real I can conceive of—as a hypothesis (or "imaginarization") establishing a relation of highest possible fidelity to the basic presuppositions of non-philosophy—is a location that appears to be a *point* of gravity around which the world revolves and is relentlessly involved by. At the same time, this "involvement"—or, rather, engagement—implies a responsibility in, of, and for both instances, the "worldly" and the "real." In other words, this theory does not propose a contention about two parallel realities, severed from each other, in which case they would plainly introduce a constitutive division into the radically immanent self. Such an argument undermines the Laruellian theoretical construct as a whole, in which we encounter the repeated claim that the real should not be taken, in any context or mode, as a metainstance with respect to the world (or to the Stranger). Divisionism and dualism are precisely what non-philosophy strives to bypass as a recourse of thought and to surpass as a discursive reality.

The real is the hearth of the human of the world; it is her or his most intimate dwelling, the "place" where he or she reappears as human-in-human, while, on the other hand, the hearth is *always already* inhabited by the person of the world.

Let us return to the quotation stating that one lives the destiny of the world through the solitary experience of living one's own individual destiny of a Stranger. And the following question surfaces: can this personal and experiential "processing of the world"—through the inevitable acts of reflection and the unique interpretations performed by the estranged instance of the "subject" (or by the Stranger)—offer a critique of and proffer ideas about the world's possible changes? I would argue not only that this is possible, but also that it is the only way of participating in the re-creation of the world that bears the weight of legitimacy and authority provided by the engaging presence of the real. The (estranged) human inevitably reflects—he or she always already assumes the status of a thinking subject or agency—(on) the ou-topos of the real, which has a priori been left behind by the necessary and inevitable stepping into the topos of the transcendental.

This ou-topos that the thinking human attempts to grasp is a nonplace in the sense of the impossibility of its being inhabited without being simultaneously *translated* by and onto the plane of the transcendental. It is a nonplace in the sense of its inaccessibility for both the (always already thinking) subject (of the estranged self) and the other to whom it is inevitably mediated by the Stranger (namely, the transcendental). The "ou" (= "u") of this u-topia refers only to the impossibility of *its being there*, without the concurrent autoimposing of the imperative for an instantaneous translation of that certain "being there" into and for the world. This action is performed by the Stranger.

The (thinking) subject reflects on that construction that we call here the "world" in an attempt to find a more adequate, better fitting, or less discomforting placement for her or his estranged existence and, together with it, for her or his nonestranged real or the human-in-human. Or rather, the Stranger negotiates with the world about his or her own position in it, as well as that of its underlying vulnerability called (by Laruelle) the "human-in-human." Through these negotiations, by insisting on a less constraining and a more pleasure generating—and thus less painful—embedment within it, the Stranger inevitably reshapes the world.

The Stranger (we all are) is compelled to situate herself or himself into one of the—at least—two gender identities stipulated by the world. The stipulations of normative gender formations—performing a normalizing and disciplinary role—have a constraining effect both on the imaginative flux of the transcendental and on the "tender flesh" of the radical immanence. Furthermore, the gender identity (just as well as any other identity produced by and participating in the world), that normative formation, aims to "tame" the unruly human-in-human precisely through putting into a linguistic grid that which is beyond language and meaning, namely, the body and, in particular, its sexual topology. This automatic urge for "taming through meaning" becomes even more compelling when femaleness—or the determination of human as female—is concerned. Birth, pregnancy, and the silent presence of secondary sexual organs and bodily marks call for the extent of the control imposed by thought (through assigning meaning) to be larger, and for a higher degree of discipline to be imposed by the world and philosophy on that elusive, material abundance of the feminine body. The higher mass of physicality, of "materiality," calls for stronger measures of discipline to be imposed by the world, that is to say, for the subjection of that organic and fluid mess to signification and conceptual order.

Certainly, "materiality" is a concept. What the world attempts to appropriate and subjugate by converting it into a concept is that which is ultimately elusive to meaning and language, that which belongs to the mute territory of the self beyond language: the real. The mute and so overwhelmingly organic present female body is that disturbing real controlled through a surplus (vis-à-vis the male body) of signification. Thought and world—perennially ruled by "Strangers inhabiting male bodies"—are compelled to capture that utter being there of the palpably different female body and the self that is imagined to inhabit it. Experienced at the very threshold of the transcendental, anterior to any workings of the rational and the processes of "relativization" that are possible only within the complexity of discursive cosmologies, this difference is perceived as radical. By virtue of its natural or "natural" inseparability from the identities assigned by the world, the particular body, "inhabited" by a particular ego-in-ego, or simply lived as yet another situating of a particular real, is dragged into a particular form of identitary subjection.

Organic or corporeal occurrences (events) are the most immediate experience (of oneself) that one can have without any intervention of the transcendental or immanently independently from and resistant to the plane of mediation (transcendence). The sense of inescapable situatedness in one's own body, the organic self-enclosure and corporeal self-circumscription, is the most direct experience of the real of one's inevitable situatedness in oneself. It is in the body that one is bound to persist in and survive as one(self), regardless of the processes of transcendence. Even if the body undergoes a series of transfigurations—also through technological interventions—it is still a matter of survival of that particular organic individuality. The body is the site of that mute persistence of a self. It is the site of the prelinguistic sensations of the real of an ego-in-ego.

Thus, the gender identity not only pertains to the real (the identity in the last instance) but also—and even more so—is necessitated by it, in the sense in which the real of the organic femaleness impels its own signification (and, hence, disciplining through identity). It is one of the creations of the world, part of the workings of the transcendental, that aim to re-present the real of femaleness and maleness. The possibilities for different (gender) identity configurations and constant refigurations that our mute, vulnerable, and insufficient bodies inevitably live in seem to be virtually numberless. And it is precisely this potentiality that not only allows but also urges the Stranger to constantly negotiate her or his position in the world.

Still, the negotiations take place within the horizon of the existing discursive realities, using the potentialities provided by the available discursiveness and the voids from within situations—made possible through the already existing language—as the "places" of origin for entirely new truths and refigurations of the world. Again, the novel truths and radical refigurations of the world are constructed with the language that undergoes certain changes, which are radically significant on the microlevel of the singularity of a particular use, and virtually imperceptible on the macrolevel of the linguistic cosmos. The possibility of utter arbitrariness in the refigurations of the identities given by the world is excluded. It is excluded by the very limitations imposed by the world (as it is). In this case, the given reality of the world—no matter how changing and dynamic—enacts, in a discrete way,[33] the role of the real. Namely, it imposes itself as the limit that cannot be dismissed, penetrated, removed, or overcome from within its actual spatio-temporal coordinates. Anything outside the coordinates of the philosophically generated world is outside the world; it is in the nowhere of the namelessness.

The Stranger who is also a woman of this world bears the imprints of that seal (of her gender identity) upon her body and person to the very core of her utmost intimate self. Her radical immanence can be neither ultimately ignorant of nor ultimately indifferent to the (forcible) touch—or, rather, grasp—of the identitary constraints, which aim to do precisely that, reach and subjugate the real of her femaleness. Her ego-in-ego, which is the home of the lived, cannot be disinterested toward and untouched by the enforcement of identitary subjugation and its laws (of subjection, control, and discipline). And even though the radical immanence is preconceptual, it is inconceivable that it can be insensitive and insensate regarding the real of the constraining effect that—through our gender identity—is perpetuated by the world. The real of our utmost self may be indifferent to the philosophical directives that are immanent to the identity construction. In the last instance, however, it cannot escape the relentless subjection to the state of enduring the regulatory hold of the world.

GLOSSARY

This glossary contains the central non-philosophical theoretical operations in the book.

Chôra. Philosophical universes, concepts organized in coherent unities establishing a (philosophical) reality in its own right, are dismantled as such (as organized wholes, universes) and their conceptual content is reduced to mere "transcendental material"—*chôra*. The "transcendental material" at hand can be used without the obligation to follow the rules of its use dictated by a doctrine, a system of thought, or a school of thought.

Human-in-Human. The human-in-human is the real of humanity. It is the radically human or the human without humanism.

Identity (or identity in the last instance). It is yet another name for the real behind a "transcendental creation," the immanence that affects the determination in the last instance of a reality. It is a concrete, specific, and unique real that affects a concrete and unique reality. It is not an abstraction or generalization of the instance of the real. That is why its determination in the last instance varies. For example, "labor force," "sexual desire," and "victim" are determinations in the last instance established in accordance with the syntax of the real, which is never abstract and general but always concrete, as are its determinations in the last instance.

The One. The one is one of the "first names" of the real. As with the other "first names," the name of the one refers to an inalienable or immanent aspect of the real. It is not a transcendental interpretation of the real but an effect of its immanence. Because of the unilaterality of the real, it necessarily and unavoidably affects thought as "the one."

The Real. In non-philosophy, the real is that which is outside interpretation, outside the cognitively created reality. It is exteriority par excellence, which is neither material nor ideal. It is the instance of radical immanence as opposed to transcendence or language. Its use is similar to Lacan's use of the term yet different, as non-Euclidean geometry is similar yet different from Euclidean geometry.

Vision-in-One. It is a nonrelationally established posture of thought that does not presuppose reciprocity between thought and the real, but rather presupposes the unilaterality of the real.

Unilateralization. Another word for "unilateralization" is "dualysis" ("dualyse"). Both terms refer to the procedure whereby the coupling of a philosophical concept and the real is radically affirmed only in order to enable a vision of each of the instances in their unilaterality, that is, beyond the logic of mutual conditioning founded upon their relation. It is a radically nonrelationist procedure of thought.

The World. It is the conceptually constructed reality that is always already transcendental and philosophical. It is similar to the notion of the "discursively constructed" reality or the language as reality in poststructuralist theory, yet fundamentally different. The non-philosophical treatment of the "world" presupposes an experienced real behind it that could and should be theoretically accounted for.

NOTES

Unless otherwise indicated, all translations in the text are mine.

FOREWORD: GENDER FICTION

1. [Translator's note] Laruelle marks a difference between *vectoriel* and *vecto-rial*. The first is translated as "vectorial" in English, whereas the second does not truly exist in French. The difference is a play on Heidegger's own "existen-tial" and "existentiell." Following follows Drew S. Burk, I have translated this as "ontovectorial." Laruelle, *Photo-Fiction, a Non-Standard Aesthetics*, trans. Drew S. Burk (Minneapolis: Univocal Publishing, 2012).
2. [Translator's note] English in original.

INTRODUCTION

1. None of those considered the founding figures of this movement (Ray Brassier, Quentin Meillassoux, Ian Hamilton Grant, Graham Harman, and Alberto Toscano) openly endorse the term "speculative realism." Nonethe-less, its circulation has been well established in the last six years, a period in which it has been used to refer to a variety of theoretical and philosophical strands derived primarily from the works of Alain Badiou, Slavoj Žižek, and François Laruelle. Although derived from diverse thinkers, they nevertheless share two common objectives: refuting the postmodern and poststructural-ist claims (a) that the real is unthinkable and (b) that thought is closed off within itself without the possibility of accessing "immanence" or explaining external reality. See Levi Bryant, Nick Srnicek, and Graham Harman, eds., *The Speculative Turn: Continental Materialism and Realism* (Melbourne:

Re.Press Publishing, 2011), 1–19. Generally speaking, the notion of the real used in the new realist theoretical and philosophical trends draws on the Lacanian conceptualization of the real and represents a reappropriation, a reinterpretation of its Lacanian core. For example, Laruelle's non-philosophy is based on what he calls a "Euclidean" reading of the real found in Lacan's psychoanalysis. The "Euclidian" twist of Laruelle's use of the Lacanian legacy of thinking the real is presented further in this introductory chapter.

2. Quentin Meillassoux, *After Finitude: An Essay on the Necessity of Contingency*, trans. Ray Brassier (London: Continuum, 2008), 79.

3. Slavoj Žižek, "Da capo senza fine," in *Contingency, Hegemony, Universality: Contemporary Dialogues on the Left*, by Judith Butler, Ernesto Laclau, and Slavoj Žižek (London: Verso, 2000), 223.

4. For example, the subject is a function in the signifying chain, where, as the Symbolic, the Imaginary and the Real are distinct in substance (what they are "made of").

5. Alain Badiou, *Being and Event* (London: Continuum, 2005), 173–175.

6. It is a concept that is the determination in the last instance of a particular reality, a concept rid of the relations that it might establish with other concepts or conceptual structures within a system of thought, a concept transcendentally impoverished. See François Laruelle, *Introduction au non-marxisme* (Paris: Presses Universitaires de France, 2000), 46–47.

7. Ibid., 21, 66.

8. François Laruelle, *Philosophie et non-philosophie* (Liège: Pierre Mardaga, 1989), 42.

9. Laruelle, *Introduction au non-marxisme*, 21.

10. The human without the humanist representation or interpretation, the human seen in its unilateral aspect of the indifferent real, is an idea present in the entire non-philosophical opus of Laruelle and is elaborated in greater detail in Laruelle, *Théorie des Étrangers: Science des hommes, démocratie et non-psychanalyse* (Paris: Éditions Kimé, 1995).

11. Laruelle, *Philosophie et non-philosophie*, 231.

12. Both "amphibology" and "mixture" are used to define the overlapping between the real and thought, which results in the mutual canceling of each other.

13. Laruelle, *Philosophie et non-philosophie*, 42ff.

14. Laruelle, *Introduction au non-marxisme*, 46–47.

15. In *Philosophie et non-philosophie*, Laruelle uses the term "cosmology" in the sense of a "conceptual universe" or "linguistic universe," a specific philosophy

that aspires to the status of "the image" of "the truth of the world" or of "the true world."

16. Laruelle, *Philosophie et non-philosophie*, 45ff.

1. ON THE ONE AND ON THE MULTIPLE

1. Marilyn Friedman, "Autonomy and Social Relationships: Rethinking the Feminist Critique," in *Feminists Rethink the Self*, ed. Diana Tietjens Meyers (New York: Westview Press, 1997), 41.
2. Ibid., 42.
3. Rosi Braidotti, *Metamorphoses: Towards a Materialist Theory of Becoming* (Cambridge: Polity Press, 2002), 39.
4. Ibid., 39–40.
5. Ibid., 40.
6. Ibid., 41.
7. Ibid., 39 (italics mine).
8. Katerina Kolozova and Zarko Trajanoski, eds., *Conversations with Judith Butler* (Skopje: Euro-Balkan Press, 2001), 29.
9. Ibid., 27–28.
10. Jane Flax, "The End of Innocence," in *Feminists Theorize the Political*, ed. Judith Butler and Joan W. Scott (London: Routledge, 1992), 454.
11. François Laruelle, *Philosophie et non-philosophie* (Liège: Pierre Mardaga, 1989), 17.
12. Ibid., 17: "C'est son auto-position fondamentale; ce que l'on peut appeler aussi son auto-factualisation ou son auto-fétichisation—tout ce que nous rassemblons sous le Principe de philosophie suffisante (PPS)."
13. François Laruelle, *Future Christ: A Lesson in Heresy*, trans. Anthony Paul Smith (London: Continuum, 2010), xxvi.
14. Laruelle, *Philosophie et non-philosophie*, 21ff.
15. Ibid., 42: "L'Un est une Identité *non-thétique* en général, c'est-à-dire à la fois non-décisionnelle (de) soi et non-positionnelle (de) soi: sans volonté pour essence, sans topologie pour existence ; sans le combat pour moteur, sans l'espace ou la figure pour manifestation . . . l'Un est le minimum transcendantal, la pétition minimale de réalité—c'est-à-dire la réalité que suppose toute pétition en général."
16. In *Undoing Gender*, Judith Butler invokes, or rather, reclaims, the notion of "I," which, nonetheless, seems to function in the text as synonymous with the concept of "subject." She writes of the "constitutive sociality of the self " and

of the "fundamental sociality of the embodied life." See Judith Butler, *Undoing Gender* (London: Routledge, 2004), 19–22.

17. In the following quotation from Jacques Lacan, one can see the distinction between the terms of *je et le sujet* and their operational statuses in the theory: "la matrice symbolique où le *je* se précipite en une forme primordiale, avant qu'il ne s'objective dans la dialectique de l'identification à l'autre et que le language ne lui restitue dans l'universel sa fonction de sujet." The term "moi" appears as a grammatical flexion of *je*, but also as a term with a more specific denotation of representing the function of the imaginary in the subject formation, or simply the location of the Imaginary in the psychic "space." Jacques Lacan, "Le stade du miroir comme formateur de la fonction du Je," in *Ecrits I* (Paris: Éditions du Seuil, 1999), 93.

18. Judith Butler, *Psychic Life of Power* (Stanford: Stanford University Press, 1997).

19. Ibid., 87.

20. Ibid.

21. Ibid., 86.

22. Ibid.

23. Ibid., 86–87.

24. Ibid., 86.

25. Ibid., 87.

26. Ibid., 88.

27. Ibid., 89.

28. Butler, *Undoing Gender*, 3.

29. Butler, *Psychic Life of Power*, 90.

30. Ibid., 89.

31. Ibid.

32. Ibid.

33. Michel Foucault, *The History of Sexuality*, vol. 3, *The Care of the Self*, trans. Robert Hurley (London: Penguin, 1990).

34. Butler, *Psychic Life of Power*, 90–91.

35. The chapter is entitled "Subjection, Resistance, Resignification: Between Freud and Foucault."

36. Michel Foucault, *The History of Sexuality*, vol. 1, *The Will to Knowledge*, trans. Robert Hurley (London: Penguin, 1998).

37. Foucault, *History of Sexuality*, 1:95–96.

38. Butler, *Psychic Life of Power*, 99.

39. Ibid., 86, 88–89, 98ff.

40. Foucault, *History of Sexuality*, 1:95–96.

41. Ibid., 1:96.

42. Ibid., 1:96.

43. Butler, *Psychic Life of Power*, 88.

44. "If I have any agency, it is opened up by the fact that I am constituted by a social world I never chose. That my agency is riven with paradox does not mean it is impossible. It means only that paradox is the condition of its possibility." Butler, *Undoing Gender*, 3.

45. Butler, *Psychic Life of Power*, 89.

46. See Michel Foucault, "Nietzsche, Genealogy, History," in *Language, Counter-Memory, Practice: Selected Essays and Interviews*, ed. D. F. Bouchard (Ithaca: Cornell University Press, 1977), 147–148.

47. Butler, *Undoing Gender*, 19.

48. Ibid., 18.

49. Ibid.

50. Gilles Deleuze, *Différence et répétition* (Paris: Presses Universitaires de France, 1993).

51. I have written more extensively on Nietzsche's conceptualization of autoreflexivity and the formation of the subject in terms of "the Will's turning against itself." See Katerina Kolozova, "Niče i poststrukturalističke teorije subjektiviteta: Čitanje kroz Judith Butler" [Nietzsche and the poststructuralist theories of subjectivity: A reading through Judith Butler], *Treća* 2 (2000): 131–138.

52. Butler, *Psychic Life of Power*, 63ff.

2. ON THE REAL AND THE IMAGINED

1. Judith Butler, *Bodies That Matter* (London: Routledge, 1993).

2. I am referring to a paragraph in *Gender Trouble* where Judith Butler writes of "social determinism" while making the following observation: "The controversy of the meaning of *construction* appears to founder on the conventional philosophical polarity between the free will and determinism." See Judith Butler, *Gender Trouble* (London: Routledge: 1999), 12.

3. Butler, *Bodies That Matter*, 6.

4. Ibid., 4.

5. Cf. Sherry B. Ortner, "Is Female to Male as Nature to Culture?" in *Women in Culture: A Women's Studies Anthology*, ed. Lucinda Joy Peach (Malden, Mass.: Blackwell, 1998), 23–44.

6. Here I draw upon Heidegger's considerations in the section "Dasein, Erschlossenheit und Wahrheit" in *Sein und Zeit* about the long tradition of identification between Truth (*Wahrheit*) and Being (*Sein*) within Western philosophy.

7. Butler, *Bodies That Matter*, 6 (italics mine).

8. François Laruelle, *Philosophie et non-philosophie* (Liège: Pierre Mardaga, 1989), 179–212, 230–238.

9. Labeling philosophy as fundamentally Greek and Jewish has caused a number of misreadings of the essence of his argument about philosophy's radical contingency usurping the status of universality. Laruelle identifies both the Greek and the Jewish tenets of what he sees as a fundamentally defunct form of thought, philosophy. An article by Andrew McGettigan is an example of such grave misreading of the core of Laruelle's argument: McGettigan, "Fabrication Defect: François Laruelle's Philosophical Materials," *Radical Philosophy* 175 (September-October 2012).

10. Laruelle, *Philosophie et non-philosophie*, 186–212.

11. This claim is in consonance with the following insight of Jane Flax: "To view oneself as a heroic lawgiver, 'foundation builder,' neutral judge, or deconstructor who has the right to evaluate the truth claims and adequacy of all forms of knowledge places the philosopher outside of a time in which such un-self-reflexive certainty seems more like a will to power than a claim to truth." Jane Flax, *Thinking Fragments: Psychoanalysis, Feminism, and Postmodernism in the Contemporary West* (Berkeley: University of California Press), 12.

12. Gilles Deleuze, *Différence et répétition* (Paris: Presses Universitaires de France, 1993), 42.

13. Gilles Deleuze and Félix Guattari, *L'Anti-Oedipe* (Paris: Les éditions de Minuit, 1972).

14. Gilles Deleuze and Félix Guattari, *Capitalisme et Schizophrénie: Mille Plateaux* (Paris: Les éditions de Minuit, 1980).

15. Deleuze, *Différence et répétition*.

16. More specifically, it is referred to the aporia of the thought of time.

17. For more on the question of the Deleuzian *retour éternel*, see Deleuze, *Nietzsche et la philosophie* (Paris: Presses Universitaires de France, 1962), 215ff.; and Deleuze, *Différence et répétition*, 118ff.

18. Cf. Gilles Deleuze, *Le bergsonisme* (Paris: Presses Universitaires de France, 1991). His Bergsonian views are clearly stated (as Bergsonian) and exhaustively elaborated in *Différence et répétition* and *Nietzsche et la philosophie*.

19. Laruelle, *Philosophie et non-philosophie*, 17–20ff.

20. Ibid., 18: "défactualisation, défétichisation ou déposition de la décision philosophique, à sa réduction à l'état de matériau d'*origine* philosophique sans doute, mais philosophiquement inerte ou stérile. On appellera *chaos* ou *chôra*—concepts évidemment à refondre—cet état de la philosophie comme matériau stérile."

21. Ibid., 232: "Le problème de la philosophie en général vient de ce qu'elle ne pense jamais les termes dans leur spécificité, mais comme contraires, dans leurs relations, au mieux dans leurs frontières et leurs voisinages. Le *concept* de fiction désigne alors, comme tout autre, une réalité amphibologique, une limitrophie du réel, qu'elle soit au-delà de celui-ci, en deçà, ou la frontière des deux. Du rationalisme classique aux déconstructions contemporaines, la fiction est restée prise dans ce rapport de mixte, c'est-à-dire unitaire. Exclue par le réel, intériorisée en lui, l'intériorisant à son tour et de toute façon prétendant le co-déterminer, jamais elle n'a échappé à ces jeux d'entre-inhibition qui sont ceux de la philosophie avec elle même, et où elle ne fut qu'un pion parmi d'autres pour une histoire qui prétendait la dépasser."

22. François Laruelle, *Introduction au non-marxisme* (Paris: Presses Universitaires de France, 2000), 46–47.

23. Ibid., 47.

24. In the sense of the nonphilosophical, Laruellian use of the term: nonrelated, nonconditioned by a philosophical decision.

25. Laruelle, *Philosophie et non-philosophie*, 37ff.

26. Or, "la cloture gréco-unitaire de la pensé" (ibid., 8); see also ibid., 215–221.

27. Ibid., 7–10, 20–22.

28. Ibid., 42.

29. Ibid., 46.

30. According to the non-philosophical terminology, the identity is always already an identity in the last instance and, in fact, the instance of the radical, the immanent, that is to say, the real: see François Laruelle, *Théorie des identités* (Paris: Presses Universitaires de France, 1992), 93ff.

31. A Nietzschean solution is that of "an escape in advance into the fiction," says Laruelle, of solving the problem by rendering the real "engulfed" by the fiction. The first is effaced by the latter—everything is but fiction. See Laruelle, *Philosophie et non-philosophie*, 231.

32. Ibid.

33. Ibid.

34. Ibid.

35. Martin Heidegger, *Bitak i vrijeme* [Croatian translation of *Sein und Zeit*] (Zagreb: Naprijed, 1988), 240.

36. Ibid.

37. This is a Lacanian term that aims to explain the effect of the real on the signifying chain as a mere event of "intervention" of an exteriority that ultimately evades subjection to language, as a thrust of an unconceivable, characterized only by its "being there" or installing itself merely as *real*, announcing that which is untranslatable in the imaginary or language. This explication of the term surely bears marks of my own interpretation. For an insight into the original words of elaboration of the term, see Jacques Lacan, *The Seminar of Jacques Lacan, Book XI, The Four Fundamental Concepts of Psychoanalysis* (New York: W. W. Norton, 1998), 53–54.

38. Laruelle, *Philosophie et non-philosophie*, 185.

39. Ibid., 207.

40. Judith Butler, *Undoing Gender* (New York: Routledge, 2004), 25 (italics mine).

41. Ibid., 26.

42. François Laruelle, *Théorie des Étrangers: Science des hommes, démocratie et non-psychanalyse* (Paris: Éditions Kimé, 1995), 183ff.

43. Butler, *Undoing Gender*, 27.

44. Ibid.

45. Ibid., 30.

46. Ibid.

47. Ibid., 4.

48. Ibid., 30–31.

49. Ibid., 29.

3. ON THE LIMIT AND THE LIMITLESS

1. This is something that can be traced throughout the entire body of work of Jacques Derrida. One of the most salient and evident examples in this sense is Derrida, "Donner la mort," in *Jacques Derrida et la pensée du don*, ed. Jean-Michel Rabaté (Paris: Métailé-Transition, 1992).

2. Jane Flax, *Thinking Fragments: Psychoanalysis, Feminism, and Postmodernism in the Contemporary West* (London: Routledge, 1991), 196.

3. Ibid., 189.

4. Ibid., 12.

5. Jane Flax in *Thinking Fragments* speaks of the same kind of anxiety caused by the sense of absolute uncertainty, of having put into question every truth, every destabilization of any position on anything; and in the description of this ruling sense of discomfort she also uses the image of vertigo. Flax writes: "Western intellectuals cannot be immune from the profound shifts now taking place in contemporary social life. These transformations have deeply disrupted many philosophers' self-understanding and sense of certainty. One of the paradoxical consequences of this break-down is that the more the fault lines in previously unproblematic ground become apparent, the more frightening it appears to be without ground, the more we want to have some ways of understanding what is happening, and the less satisfactory the existing ways of thinking about experience become. All this results in a most uncomfortable form of intellectual vertigo to which appropriate responses are not clear." Ibid., 6.

6. Katerina Kolozova and Zarko Trajanoski, eds., *Conversations with Judith Butler* (Skopje: Euro-Balkan Press, 2001), 25–30.

7. Judith Butler, "Contingent Foundations," in *Feminist Contentions: A Philosophical Exchange*, by Seyla Benhabib, Judith Butler, Drucilla Cornell, and Nancy Fraser (London: Routledge, 1995), 36–37.

8. Jean Baudrillard, *Simbolicka razmena i smrt* [Serbo-Croatian translation of the *Symbolic Exchange and Death*] (Gornji Milanovac: Decje Novine, 1991).

9. Slavoj Žižek, *Interrogating the Real* (London: Continuum, 2006); Slavoj Žižek, *Tarrying with the Negative* (Durham: Duke University Press), 1993. I find his elaboration of the concept in Lacan and his unraveling of the theoretical potential for a political critique particularly compelling in his contributions to Judith Butler, Ernesto Laclau, and Slavoj Žižek, *Hegemony, Contingency, Universality* (London: Verso, 2000).

10. Alenka Zupančič, *The Odd One In: On Comedy* (Cambridge, Mass.: MIT Press, 2007); and Alenka Zupančič, *The Ethics of the Real* (London: Verso, 2000).

11. François Laruelle, *Future Christ: A Lesson in Heresy*, trans. Anthony Paul Smith (London: Continuum, 2010), xxvi: "Fundamental terms which symbolize the Real and its modes according to its radical immanence or its identity. They are deprived of their philosophical sense and become, via axiomatized abstraction, the terms—axioms and theorems—of non-philosophy."

12. Carl Schmitt, *Political Theology*, trans. George D. Schwab (Cambridge, Mass.: MIT Press, 1985).

13. Peter Hallward, *Badiou: A Subject to Truth* (Minneapolis: University of Minnesota Press, 2003), 120.

14. That is to say, by the instances of power and authority to accord that recognition.

15. François Laruelle, *Théorie générale des victimes* (Paris: Fayard, 2012).

16. Ibid., 40.

17. Jacques Lacan, *Écrits I* (Paris: Éditions du Seuil, 1999), 74: "Il faut alors reconnaîtreque ces cadres, loin d'avoir été forgés pour une conception objective de la réalité psychique ne sont que les produits d'une sorte d'erosion conceptuelle où se retracent les vicissitudes d'un effort spécifique qui pousse l'homme à rechercher une *garantie de vérité*: garantie qui, on le voit, est transcendante par sa position, et le reste donc dans sa forme, même quand le philosophe vient à nier son existence."

18. Ibid., 85: "Travail d'illusioniste [about psychoanalysis], nous dirait-on, s'il n'avait justement pour fruit de résoudre une illusion. Son action thérapeutique, au contraire, doit être définie essentiellement comme un double mouvement par où *l'image*, d'abord diffuse et brisée, est régressivement assimilée au réel, pour être progressivement désassimilée du réel, c'est-à-dire restaurée dans sa réalité propre. Action qui témoigne de l'efficience de cette réalité."

19. Jacques Lacan, *The Seminar of Jacques Lacan, Book XI: The Four Fundamental Concepts of Psychoanalysis*, ed. Jacques-Alain Miller, trans. Alan Sheridan (New York: W. W. Norton, 1998), 53–64.

20. Ibid., 53–54.

21. Ibid., 54.

22. Ibid., 54–55.

23. Butler, Laclau, and Žižek, *Contingency, Hegemony, Universality*.

24. Zupančič, *The Ethics of the Real*, 234.

25. François Laruelle, *Philosophie et non-philosophie* (Liège: Pierre Mardaga, 1989), 40.

26. Ibid., 50.

27. Ibid.: "On dira que c'est un Reflet non-thétique (du) réel, reflet non-spéculaire ou sans miroir, ou une description 'en dernière instance seulement' de l'Un."

28. Ibid., 12–13: "Or cette règle ultime des agrégations conceptuelles en régime philosophique n'est pas brisée, elle est épurée et devient plutôt immanente dans le sérialisme philosophique contemporain et même dans la déconstruction où l'un des opposés de la Dyade est remplacé simplement par l'Autre-qui-n'est-pas."

29. Ibid., 50: "On se gardera de dire que tout langage trahit l'Un, parce que le langage manipulerait toujours, comme c'est le cas, des couples d'opposés et serait l'élément nourricier des dualités unitaires. C'est là une pensée qui postule que le langage est reflet spéculaire de l'Un, qu'il a même structure que lui (cf. L'argument du *Tractatus*) ou lui est isomorphe. C'est le postulat de l'ontologie et de la théologie négative, c'est surtout une présupposition supplémentaire et inutile : le langage peut décrire l'Un, qui n'a pas du tout la même structure que lui, sans le refléter exactement ou le reproduire."

30. François Laruelle, *Introduction au non-marxisme* (Paris: Presses Universitaires de France, 2000), 46–47.

31. François Laruelle, *Théorie des identités* (Paris: Presses Universitaires de France, 1992), 93: "La distinction des deux objets ne recouvre pas en effet celle de l'expérience et du concept, du concret et de l'abstrait, de l'expérimentation et du théorique—ni aucune de leurs 'dialectisations' ou 'couplages.'"

32. Ibid.

33. Ibid.

34. Ibid.

35. Ibid.: "qu'une connaissance se soumet au réel et ne prétend que le 'refléter' ou le décrire à travers l'opération même de production théorico-expérimentale de ses représentations."

36. Drucilla Cornell, *The Philosophy of the Limit* (London: Routledge, 1992).

37. Ibid., 1.

38. Ibid., 71–72.

39. Ibid., 71.

4. THE REAL TRANSCENDING ITSELF (THROUGH LOVE)

1. François Laruelle, *Anti-Badiou: Sur l'introduction du maoïsme dans la philosophie* (Paris: Éditions Kimé, 2011).

2. Peter Hallward, *Badiou: A Subject to Truth* (Minneapolis: University of Minnesota Press, 2003), 250.

3. François Laruelle, *Philosophie et non-philosophie* (Liège: Pierre Mardaga, 1989), 168.

4. Hallward, *Badiou*, 250.

5. Laruelle, *Philosophie et non-philosophie*, 168.

6. Katerina Kolozova, "Theories of the Immanent Rebellion: Non-Marxism and Non-Christianity," in *Laruelle and Non-Philosophy*, ed. John Mullarkey

and Anthony Paul Smith (Edinburgh: Edinburgh University Press, 2012), 209–226.

7. Marguerite Porete, *The Mirror of the Simple Souls*, trans. Ellen L. Babinsky (Mahwah, N.J.: Paulist Press, 1993).

8. Laruelle, *Philosophie et non-philosophie*, 97.

9. François Laruelle, *Théorie des identités* (Paris: Presses Universitaires de France, 1992).

10. Ibid., 93: "Bien que fondée comme pouvoir absolu (quoique fini) sur une immanence pure qui ne contient pas la moindre parcelle de transcendance, la science n'exclut pas définitivement celel-ci, au contraire, mais elle exige que la trenscendance des objets et de ses représentations participe elle aussi de cette essence absolue ou de cette phénoménalité toute immanente."

11. Ibid.

12. Ibid., 149.

13. Ibid., 150.

14. Ibid., 93.

15. Nonanalysis is the nonphilosophical appropriation or Laruellian nonstandard theoretical practice of Lacanian psychoanalysis.

16. Laruelle, *Théorie des identités*, 145–150.

17. Laruelle, *Philosophie et non-philosophie*, 93–95.

18. The term far more frequently used in nonphilosophy is "nonanalysis" instead of "nonpsychoanalysis."

19. Laruelle, *Théorie des Étrangers: Science des hommes, démocratie, non-psych-analyse* (Paris: Éditions Kimé, 1998), 221–234, namely, the sections "Le Réel ou le Joui-sans-Jouissance" and "La jouissance: 1) comme organon du Réel" of chapter 3 ("Principes de la non-psychanalyse").

20. Rosi Braidotti, *Metamorphoses: Towards a Materialist Theory of Becoming* (Cambridge: Polity Press, 2002).

21. Ibid., 23 (italics mine).

22. Ibid., 119.

23. François Laruelle, *Théorie generale des victimes* (Paris: Fayard, 2012).

24. What Badiou calls a truth process or a generic procedure is, ontologically, "the coming to be of this subset, through the succession of finite investigations that 'test' the elements of the situation with respect to a supplementary element, which is the trace in the situation of the vanished event. A subject is in a sense the active face, the 'naturing nature' of these explorations, materially indiscernible from their existence." Hallward, *Badiou*, 134. Hallward's

quotation is taken from Badiou, "Platon et/ou Aristote-Leibniz: Théorie des ensembles et théorie des Topos sous l'oeil du philosophe," in *L'Objectivité mathématique: Platonismes et structures formelles*, ed. Marco Panza (Paris: Masson, 1995), 79.
25. Hallward, *Badiou*, 128–134.

5. THE REAL IN THE IDENTITY

1. Peter Hallward, *Badiou: A Subject to Truth* (Minneapolis: University of Minnesota Press, 2003), 116–122.
2. François Laruelle, *Philosophie et non-philosophie* (Liège: Pierre Mardaga, 1989), 17: "C'est son auto-position fondamentale; ce que l'on peut appeler aussi son auto-factualisation ou son auto-fétichisation—tout ce que nous rassemblons sous le *Principe de philosophie suffisante* (PPS)."
3. Ibid., 12–14.
4. It is also called nonpsychoanalysis, but the adopted technical term by Laruelle is "nonanalysis." See Laruelle, *Théorie des Étrangers* (Paris: Éditions Kimé, 1995), 172.
5. Ibid., 15.
6. Ibid., 76–77.
7. Ibid., 76.
8. Laruelle, *Philosophie et non-philosophie*, 90: "Il y a d'une part une ouverture-sans-ouvert, une extase-sans-horizon, une transcendance irréfléchie et qui reste en soi, sans donner lieu à un espace, un horizon, une position, dans lesquels elle viendrait sans coup férir se ré-inscrire et s'inhiber. On peut appeler aussi cette région de l'objectivité *l'Autre-non-thétique*."
9. Laruelle, *Théorie des Étrangers*, 77.
10. Ibid., 78.
11. François Laruelle, *Le Christ futur: Une leçon d'hérésie* (Paris: Exils Éditeur, 2002), especially the chapter "La dernière prophétie ou l'homme-messie"; English translation: François Laruelle, *Future Christ: A Lesson in Heresy*, trans. Anthony Paul Smith (London: Continuum, 2010), 113–125, "The Last Prophet or Man-Messiah."
12. Cf. Laruelle, *Ethique de l'Étranger* (Paris: Éditions Kimé, 2000), 259.
13. François Laruelle, *Théorie generale des victimes* (Paris: Fayard, 2012), 51: "Nous entendons par victimes des vécus neutralizes ou sans-vie, des Erlebnisse plutôt que des catégories d'individus même si ces vécus sont repérables

depuis ces individus. Les vécus non-individuels de l'être exploité, de l'être exclu, ceux de l'être-assassiné, de l'être-persécuté, de l'être-humilié, et non pas comme font vite l'histoire et la philosophie."

14. Laruelle, *Théorie des Étrangers*, 77: "'Humanité' proprement dite, dont nous dirons qu'elle n'est pas habitée d'Ego—l'Ego n'habite pas—mais uniquement d'Étrangers."

15. Ibid., 76: "On remarquera que l'Étranger n'est pas la relation de l'Ego avec le Monde, relation synthétique de réciprocité et de convertibilité. Mais la relation, relativement autonome, extraite du Monde (du mixte méta-humain) et qui est reçue ou vécue en-Ego ou en-Homme sans être relation à l'Ego."

16. Ibid., 164: "Ce résidu en effet ne peut pas être constitué de la seule et pure transcendance, supposée empiriquement abstraite du mixte et opposée à l'immanence de l'Ego.... Nous ne faisons pas de l'Ego un nouvel usage métaphysique et idéaliste et par conséquant nous ne disons pas seulement qu'il implique la dissolution sans reste de l'amphibologie de l'Ego et du Xenos."

17. In Laruelle's *Théorie des Étrangers*, we read: "L'Ego est si concret qu'il n'entre dans aucune relation mais peut en recevoir ou en tolérer une sur son mode propre d'Ego. C'est pourquoi l'Étranger est une dualité qui suppose l'Ego *mais qui est absolument rejetée hors de lui . . . reçue en-Identité sans constituer une partie réelle de celle-ci.*" See ibid., 70–74, 76–83, quotation from 76 (italics mine).

18. Ibid., 82.

19. Ibid., 77.

20. Ibid.

21. Ibid.

22. Ibid.

23. Ibid., 74: "l'autonomie radical (mais non exclusive) de l'Ego réel."

24. Laruelle, *Future Christ*, 6. I have written in more length on the heretic nature of the immanent revolt of the human-in-human in John Mullarkey's and Anthony Paul Smith's collection *Laruelle and Non-Philosophy* from 2012. Katerina Kolozova, "Theories of the Immanent Rebellion: Non-Marxism and Non-Christianity," in *Laruelle and Non-Philosophy*, ed. John Mullarkey and Anthony Paul Smith (Edinburgh: Edinburgh University Press, 2012), 209–226.

25. Alain Badiou, *Ethics*, trans. Peter Hallward (London: Verso, 2001), 7.

26. Hallward, *Badiou*, 120.

27. Laruelle, *Théorie des Étrangers*, 225: "Il est le vécu indivis (de) la douleur—celle-ci ne le déterminant pas—comme le vécu indivis de la joie, mais nullement leur synthèse, même immanente."

28. Ibid., 222: "Le Joui-qui-n'est-que-Joui n'est pas le résultat ou le produit de l'opération transcendante de la jouissance, il est Joui-en-Joui ou immanent (à) soi plutôt qu'à la jouissance qui le donnerait ou le constituerait."

29. I am asking this question in addition to the previous one, since I strongly disbelieve in the omnipotence of thought and the authority of cognition over the real and the messy life, and, hence, in moments of theoretical incapacitation, and following my own "theoretical identity in the last instance," I would choose to follow my sense of "just" and "unjust" (or more exactly: my preference of "caring" versus "uncaring") vis-à-vis the knowledge of "true" and "false." I also choose not to define these terms, since I need them as points of nonreflection, of noncognition, in order to preserve my own theoretical attempts from possible omnipotent pretensions or to restrain such desires that are inevitably inbuilt in any theoretical "self-investment." Within my own horizon of theoretical attempts, these points act as instances of the (Lacanian) Real.

30. Laruelle, *Future Christ*, 104.

31. Laruelle, *Théorie des Étrangers*, 224–225: "c'est que le Joui n'a pas besoin de cette symbolization, le Réel excluant par essence et positivement le signifiant."

32. François Laruelle and Anne-Françoise Schmid, "L'identité sexuée," *Identities* 2, no. 3 (2003): 55: "Le problème du rapport des sexes au génie pourrait être également déplacé. Dans son interprétation 'philosophique' habituelle, il postule la capacité de vivre en son proper destin le destin du Monde et donc se jouer des contraires et de se les donner librement. C'est la faculté de se donner le Monde et le sentiment d'être pour lui plutôt qu'en lui. La-femme passe son énergie dans le Monde, puisqu'elle en assure la stabilité. Le Monde, dessiné par les structures de la philosophie, peut être lui aussi transformé, en ce sens qu'il n'est pas nécessaire de se le donner dans son unité ni sa totalité. Il y faut une généralisation de la philosophie, sa transformation en matériau. Le génie pourrait alors apparaître sous des formes moins totalitaires et impulsives, moins masculines. C'est là aussi tout un travail de transformation des énoncés philosophiques, dont l'objet finit toujours par être quelque chose du Monde."

33. In such a "manifestation" of itself, the world establishes radical discontinuity with its immanent position, creating a functional leap of the kind where it "does the work" of the real or of the limit.

BIBLIOGRAPHY

Badiou, Alain. *Being and Event*. Translated by Oliver Feltham. London: Continuum, 2005.

———. *Ethics: An Essay on the Understanding of Evil*. Translated by Peter Hallward. London: Verso, 2001.

———. *Infinite Thought: Truth and the Return to Philosophy*. Translated by Oliver Feltham and Justin Clemens. London: Continuum, 2003.

———. *Manifesto for Philosophy*. Translated, edited, and with an introduction by Norman Madarasz. Albany: SUNY Press, 1999.

———. *Saint Paul: The Foundation of Universalism*. Translated by Ray Brassier. Stanford: Stanford University Press, 2003.

———. *Theoretical Writings*. Edited and translated by Ray Brassier and Alberto Toscano. London: Continuum, 2004.

Baudrillard, Jean. *The Perfect Crime*. Translated by Chris Turner. London: Verso, 1996.

———. *Simbolicka razmena i smrt* [Serbo-Croatian translation of *Symbolic Exchange and Death*]. Gornji Milanovac: Decje Novine, 1991.

———. *Simulacra and Simulation*. Translated by Sheila Faria Glaser. Ann Arbor: University of Michigan Press, 1995.

Benhabib, Seyla, Judith Butler, Drucilla Cornell, and Nancy Fraser. *Feminist Contentions: A Philosophical Exchange*. London: Routledge, 1995.

Bergson, Henri. *Matière et mémoire: Essai sur la relation du corps à l'ésprit*. Paris: Presses Universitaires de France, 1993. Originally published in 1896.

———. *La pensée et le mouvant*. Paris: Presses Universitaires de France, 1946.

Braidotti, Rosi. *Metamorphoses: Towards a Materialist Theory of Becoming*. Cambridge: Polity Press, 2002.

———. *Nomadic Subjects: Embodiment and Sexual Difference in Contemporary Feminist Theory*. New York: Columbia University Press, 1994.

Brassier, Ray. *Nihil Unbound: Enlightenment and Extinction.* New York: Palgrave Macmillan, 2007.

Butler, Judith. *Antigone's Claim: Kinship Between Life and Death.* New York: Columbia University Press, 2002.

——. *Bodies That Matter: On the Discursive Limits of "Sex."* London: Routledge, 1993.

——. *Frames of War: When Is Life Grievable?* London: Verso, 2009.

——. *Gender Trouble: Feminism and the Subversion of Identity.* London: Routledge, 1999.

——. *Precarious Life.* London: Verso, 2006.

——. *The Psychic Life of Power: Theories in Subjection.* Stanford: Stanford University Press, 1997.

——. *Undoing Gender.* London: Routledge, 2004.

Butler, Judith, Ernesto Laclau, and Slavoj Žižek. *Contingency, Hegemony, Universality: Contemporary Dialogues on the Left.* London: Verso, 2000.

Butler, Judith, and Joan Scott, eds. *Feminists Theorize the Political.* London: Routledge, 1992.

Butler, Judith, John Guillory, and Kendall Thomas, eds. *What's Left of Theory: New Work on the Politics of Literary Theory.* London: Routledge, 2000.

Campbell, Kirsten. *Jacques Lacan and Feminist Epistemology.* New York: Routledge, 2004.

Cornell, Drucilla. *The Philosophy of the Limit.* New York: Routledge, 1992.

Deleuze, Gilles. *Le bergsonisme.* Paris: Presses Universitaires de France, 1993. Originally published in 1966.

——. *Différence et répétition.* Paris: Presses Universitaires de France, 1993. Originally published in 1968.

——. *Expressionism in Philosophy: Spinoza.* Translated by Martin Joughin. New York: Zone Books, 1990.

——. *Foucault.* Translated and edited by Sean Hand. London: Athlone Press, 1999.

——. *Logique du sens.* Paris: Les éditions de Minuit, 1969.

——. *Nietzsche et la philosophie.* Paris: Presses Universitaires de France, 1962.

——. *Pure Immanence: Essays on a Life.* Translated by Anne Boyman. New York: Zone Books, 2001.

Deleuze, Gilles, and Felix Guattari. *L'Anti-Oedipe.* Paris: Les éditions de Minuit, 1972.

——. *Capitalisme et Schizophrénie: Mille Plateaux.* Paris: Les éditions de Minuit, 1980.

Derrida, Jacques. *Apories*. Paris: Galilée, 1996.

———. *Dissemination*. Translated by Barbara Johnson. Chicago: University of Chicago Press, 1981.

———. "Donner la mort." In *L'ethique du don: Jacques Derrida et la pensée du don*, edited by Jean-Michel Rabaté. Paris: Métailé-Transition, 1992.

———. *L'écriture et la difference*. Paris: Éditions du Seuil, 1967.

———. *Margins of Philosophy*. Translated by Alan Bass. Chicago: University of Chicago Press, 1984.

———. *Of Sprit: Heidegger and the Question*. Translated by Geoffrey Bennington and Rachel Bowlby. Chicago: University of Chicago Press, 1991.

Flax, Jane. *Disputed Subjects: Essays on Psychoanalysis, Politics and Philosophy*. London: Routledge, 1993.

———. *Thinking Fragments: Psychoanalysis, Feminism, and Postmodernism in the Contemporary West*. London: Routledge, 1991.

Foucault, Michel. *Discipline and Punish*. Translated by Alan Sheridan. London: Penguin, 1991.

———. *The History of Sexuality*. Vol. 1, *The Will to Knowledge*. Translated by Robert Hurley. London: Penguin, 1998.

———. *The History of Sexuality*. Vol. 2, *The Use of Pleasure*. Translated by Robert Hurley. London: Penguin, 1992.

———. *The History of Sexuality*. Vol. 3, *The Care of the Self*. Translated by Robert Hurley. London: Penguin, 1990.

———. *Madness and Civilization: A History of Insanity in the Age of Reason*. Translated by Richard Howard. New York: Vintage, 1973.

———. "Nietzsche, Genealogy, History." In *Language, Counter-Memory, Practice: Selected Essays and Interviews*, edited by D. F. Bouchard. Ithaca: Cornell University Press, 1977.

Friedman, Marilyn. "Autonomy and Social Relationships: Rethinking the Feminist Critique." In *Feminists Rethink the Self*, edited by Diana Tietjens Meyers. Oxford: Westview Press, 1997.

Gibson-Graham, J. K. *The End of Capitalism (as We Knew It): A Feminist Critique of Political Economy*. Malden, Mass.: Blackwell, 1999.

Hallward, Peter. *Badiou: A Subject to Truth*. Minneapolis: University of Minnesota Press, 2003.

Heidegger, Martin. *Bitak i vrijeme* [Croatian translation of *Sein und Zeit*]. Zagreb: Naprijed, 1988.

Huntington, Patricia J. *Ecstatic Subjects, Utopia, and Recognition: Kristeva, Heidegger, Irigaray*. Albany: SUNY Press, 1998.

Kolozova, Katerina. "Niče i poststrukturalističke teorije subjektiviteta: Čitanje kroz Judith Butler" [Nietzsche and the poststructuralist theories of subjectivity: A reading through Judith Butler]. *Treća* 2 (2000): 131–138.

———. "Theories of the Immanent Rebellion: Non-Marxism and Non-Christianity." In *Laruelle and Non-Philosophy*, edited by John Mullarkey and Anthony Paul Smith, 209–226. Edinburgh: Edinburgh University Press, 2012.

———. "Les troubles et metamorphoses de Mnemosyne." *Monitor: Journal of the Institutum Studiorum Humanitatis* 1/2 (2003): 17–33.

Kolozova, Katerina, and Zarko Trajanoski, eds. *Conversations with Judith Butler*. Skopje: Euro-Balkan Press, 2001. This is a bilingual edition in English and Macedonian.

Lacan, Jacques. *Écrits 1*. Paris: Éditions du Seuil, 1999. Originally published in 1966.

———. *Encore: The Seminar of Jacques Lacan, Book XX: On Feminine Sexuality, the Limits of Love and Knowledge*. Edited by Jacques-Alain Miller. Translated with notes by Bruce Fink. New York: W. W. Norton, 1999.

———. *Les quatres concepts fondamentaux de la psychanalyse*. Edited by Jacques-Alain Miller. Paris: Éditions de Seuil, 1973.

———. *The Seminar of Jacques Lacan, Book I: Freud's Papers on Technique*. Edited by Jacques-Alain Miller. Translated with notes by John Forrester. New York: W. W. Norton, 1988.

———. *The Seminar of Jacques Lacan, Book XI: The Four Fundamental Concepts of Psychoanalysis*. Edited by Jacques-Alain Miller. Translated by Alan Sheridan. New York: W. W. Norton, 1998.

Laruelle, François. *Anti-Badiou: Sur l'introduction du maoïsme dans la philosophie*. Paris: Éditions Kimé, 2011.

———. *Ethique de l'Etranger*. Paris: Éditions Kimé, 2000.

———. *Future Christ: A Lesson in Heresy*. Translated by Anthony Paul Smith. London: Continuum, 2010. English translation of *Le Christ futur: Une leçon d'hérésie*. Paris: Exils Éditeur, 2002.

———. *Introduction au non-marxisme*. Paris: Presses Universitaires de France, 2000.

———. *La lutte et l'utopie à la fin des temps philosophiques*. Paris: Éditions Kimé, 2004.

———. *Philosophie et non-philosophie*. Liège: Pierre Mardaga, 1989.

———. *Théorie des Étrangers: Science des hommes, démocratie et non-psychanalyse*. Paris: Éditions Kimé, 1995.

———. *Théorie des identités*. Paris: Presses Universitaires de France, 1992.

———. *Théorie generale des victimes*. Paris: Fayard, 2012.

Laruelle, François, and Anne-Françoise Schmid. "L'identité sexuée." *Identities* 2, no. 3 (2003): 49–61.

Lowe, Jonathan E. *Subjects of Experience*. Cambridge: Cambridge University Press, 1996.

Meillassoux, Quentin. *After Finitude: An Essay on the Necessity of Contingency*. Translated by Ray Brassier. London: Continuum, 2008. English translation of *Après la finitude: Essai sur la nécessité de la contingence*. Paris: Seuil, 2006.

Meyers, Diana Tietjens, ed. *Feminists Rethink the Self*. Oxford: Westview Press, 1997.

——. *Subjection and Subjectivity: Psychoanalytic Feminism and Moral Philosophy*. London: Routledge, 1994.

Mullarkey, John, and Anthony Paul Smith, eds. *Laruelle and Non-Philosophy*. Edinburgh: Edinburgh University Press, 2012.

Porete, Marguerite. *The Mirror of the Simple Souls*. Translated by Ellen L. Babinsky. Mahwah, N.J.: Paulist Press, 1993.

Rosset, Clément. *Le réel: Traité de l'idiotie*. Paris: Les éditions de Minuit, 1978.

Siebers, Tobin. *The Subject and Other Subjects: On Ethical, Aesthetic, and Political Identity*. Ann Arbor: University of Michigan Press, 2001.

Žižek, Slavoj, ed. *Cogito and the Unconscious*. Durham: Duke University Press, 1998.

——. "Da capo senza fine." In Butler, Laclau, and Žižek, *Contingency, Hegemony, Universality*, 213–262.

——. *The Sublime Object of Ideology*. London: Verso, 1989.

——. *The Ticklish Subject: The Absent Center of Political Ontology*. London: Verso, 1999.

Zupančič, Alenka. *The Ethics of the Real: Kant and Lacan (Wo Es War)*. London: Verso, 2000.

INDEX

"gréco-judaïque" foundation of philosophy, 58, 95
grief, 10, 127–29
Guattari, Félix, 60

Hegelian idealism, 99
Heidegger, Martin, 59, 71–72, 157n1 (forward), 162n6
The History of Sexuality, The Care of the Self (Foucault), 42–44
the human and human-in-human, 155; immanent revolt, 170n24; Laruelle, xi, xv, 90, 94, 158n10; and radical solitude, 108, 118; and the real, 103, 110–11, 113–15, 124, 128, 132; transcendence, 136–38, 140–42, 144, 146; and the world, 148, 150–52

the "I," 27, 32–36, 46–50, 71, 76, 117, 159n16
"L'identité sexuée" (Laruelle and Schmid), 148–49
identity, 155; Alain Badiou, 104; François Laruelle, 64–65, 94, 97, 108–10, 113, 118, 165n11; gender, 32, 37, 53, 57, 118, 148, 152–54; and love, 119, 124–25; and political rights, 16, 73, 171n29; poststructuralist theories, 163n30; and the real, 131–38, 140–48, 165n11; and the subject, 34, 39–40
the Imaginary, 36–37, 66–69, 82, 117, 158n4, 160n17
Innerweltliche Seiende (in-the-world-existent, Heidegger), 71
Introduction au nonmarxisme (Laruelle), 9
Irigaray, Luce, 25, 106, 116–18

je et le sujet, 160n17. *See also* the "I"; the subject

Kantian ideas, 2, 21, 51–52

labor force, 17, 27–28, 155
Lacan, Jacques: Drucilla Cornell on, 98–99; function, 2; the Imaginary, 66, 68; psychoanalysis, 33–34, 36, 168n16; the real, 9, 67–68, 85, 91–94, 157–58n1; the subject and the "I," 33–34, 160n17; trauma, 9; truth, 91
language: and the body, 53–54, 152–53; and identity, 132–33, 135–36; and the limit, 85–88; and love, 122–24, 126, 128–29; and preservation of the self, 48–50; and the real, 36–38, 67–71, 93–102, 104–8, 111–17, 148–49; and thought, 99–102
L'Anti-Oedipe (Deleuze and Guatarri), 60, 80
Laruelle, François, 106; Christology, 3; cloning, 9; cosmology, 158n15; decisionism, 6, 9, 133; dichotomy and dualism, 28–32, 59, 62–63; empathy or compassion, 123; gender, ix–xvi, 106, 148–51; gréco-judaïque basis of philosophy, 58, 162n9; the human, 90, 135–37, 158n10; Lacanian psychoanalysis, 157–58n1; the limit, 72; "non-" prefix, 4; the one, 94–97; poststructuralist feminism, 106; queer theory, 106; the radical, 103–5, 108–9; the real, 9, 58–59, 72, 94–97, 112, 139–42; resistance, 72; the scientific, 3, 108–9; speculative realism, 157n1 (intro.); the

INSURRECTIONS: CRITICAL STUDIES IN RELIGION, POLITICS, AND CULTURE

Slavoj Žižek, Clayton Crockett, Creston Davis, Jeffrey W. Robbins, Editors